Teen Boy's Success Book

The Ultimate Self-Help Book for Boys; Everything You Need to Know to Become a Man

Mike Stone

Contents

Published by Black Line Press

Author contact: mikestone114@yahoo.com

Introduction

Your Journey Starts Here

You're going to encounter some mind-blowing information in this book; information that no one else has ever told you before and that no one else will ever tell you again. How you process that information is up to you. You can dismiss it without cause . . . or embrace it and become a man.

From this day forward, you'll know exactly what it takes to become a man. You'll know what's expected of you and how to begin planning the remainder of your life. Consider today to be the dividing point between your time on this earth as a boy and your time on this earth as a man.

Inside this book you'll find ten important steps to master—one per chapter. Master these ten steps and you'll be a man, no matter what your age. In fact, you don't even have to master the ten steps. Just become better than average in them, because here's a secret: most adult men never master all ten. Most adult men are lucky if they master only two of these ten steps. Only a few men have mastered more than five of them and I've never met a man who has mastered all ten.

Here's another secret: men today are a pathetic lot. They're weak facsimiles of real men, obsessed with tattoos, steroids, and phony posturing. It's all pretend masculinity. They sit like drooling retards in front of the boob tube, believing every lie they're told, watching sports, and simping to pornography.

The almost complete feminization of modern men has made it easy for a real man (you) to shine. With only a little effort on your part, you can surpass all of these simps and weaklings, and position yourself as a man of power.

I don't care what your current age is. Begin studying and mastering the ten steps in this book and it won't take long for you to pass every adult male in your life in terms of manhood. You'll stand head and shoulders above them all. You'll be a man among men.

So here's your key to success . . . read every word of this book and do your best at mastering these ten steps. In return, I promise to give it to you straight in the pages of this book. I'm going to explain to you in simple language the way life *really* works. It's not what you've been taught in school and it's not what you've heard from any other person. If any of this appears daunting, cheer up. As a reader of this book, you can contact me at any time for any reason and I'll be happy to help you or answer any question you have.

Over the next few minutes, you're going to read things that will leave you stunned, breathless, and eager for more. Reality as you know it is about to be turned upside down.

Are you ready to take that journey? If so, then I invite you now to come along for the ride of your life. The first step is easy. Simply turn to the next page.

Chapter One

Being Polite Can Save Your Life

The gun cracked twice. Loud reports that echoed in my ears. The car ahead of me swerved suddenly and I had to slam on my brakes and swerve my own car to avoid hitting it. The car where the shots came from sped off.

I later learned that the driver of the car ahead of me was dead. So was a two-year-old child strapped to a car seat. When apprehended, the shooter claimed the dead driver had cut him off in traffic. It was a typical case of road rage, where a little politeness could have saved two lives.

Fiction vs. Reality

Nobody likes a smartass.

Now if you read popular fiction or watch television, you might think just the opposite. That's because popular fiction and television are filled with obnoxious, wisecracking characters that are made to look cool and hip. Young adult novels and television shows aimed at young people are filled with that type of character.

But here's the thing with all of those books and shows: they have no basis in reality. They're written by whiny, know-nothing writers with little life experience.

The people who write and produce those books and television shows create characters that reflect who they are as people—or rather who they wish they were. They think being rude is funny, but they wouldn't dare talk or act that way in real life. If they did, they'd get a punch in the mouth or worse. So they hide behind the characters they create.

After a while, all of these fictional characters from all of these whiny writers start to sound alike. And why wouldn't they? They're all coming from the same basic mold: an insecure, cowardly writer. These writers have never experienced anything remotely close to what they're writing about, so they make it all up. That's why everything they write rings hollow and false, including and especially the obnoxious, wise-cracking characters that populate their books and television shows.

You'll notice that the best writers of young adult fiction don't do this. It's only the mediocre ones. Take S.E. Hinton, the author of *Rumble Fish* and *The Outsiders*. The characters in Hinton's books are troubled, introspective teens. I suspect that Hinton is also troubled and introspective as her books are rooted in reality and ring true when you read them. Hinton isn't faking it, like most other writers.

The average reader and television viewer has as little life experience as the average writer. So naturally, they think these whiny, obnoxious characters are cool and hip, and they imitate them. Then they wonder why some guy they just insulted hauls off and belts them. Or in some cases, pulls out a gun and shoots. In that case they're no longer wondering. They're dead.

You Get What You Give Out

The one factor that separates men from boys more than any other is maturity. And one of the hallmarks of maturity is politeness. To be a man, you must be polite.

Being polite is not only civilized behavior it's also in your best interest. That's because humans are hardwired to reciprocate behavior. If you show someone respect, they'll show you respect back. That's how life works.

There are exceptions. Every now and then you'll encounter an ill-mannered jerk who won't reciprocate your respect, or a low-level animal type with no impulse control who only understands brute force. But for the most part, people will treat you the same way you treat them. Therefore, to function effectively in life, you must be polite.

Being polite will make you stand out, because most people aren't doing it. When you're polite to somebody that no one else is polite to, such as a clerk in a store, a government employee, or a police officer, they will bend over backwards to help you.

Being polite has other hidden benefits. People are killed every day due to real or perceived slights of respect, everything from driving rudely in traffic to a simple flick of the eyes. People have been killed over both of those things. I've seen it happen. So being polite isn't only about being nice or civilized, it may just save your life.

Seven Magic Words to Open Any Door

The key to politeness rests in seven magic words; seven words that will open practically any door. Those seven words are "please," "thank you," "excuse me," and "I'm sorry."

These seven words pack a wallop of power. Use them generously.

Say please when you ask someone for help or for a favor, and they will be much more likely to do what you're asking than if you don't say please.

Say thank you when someone provides you with help or does you a favor.

Say thank you when someone does something nice for you or gives you a compliment.

There's human psychology behind all of this. When you approach someone and ask for help, it frames the person you're asking as a hero or problem solver. That's a role people are eager to embrace. Everyone wants to be a hero or problem solver. It's an ego boost and a healthy one at that. When the word "please" is added to the mix, it increases their feeling of being that hero or problem solver. It makes them feel respected and they become much more apt to grant the request being asked of them.

By the same token, when someone helps another person, they like to hear the words "thank you." That's also an ego boost. It makes the person being thanked feel like they've done a good deed. It's especially important in business exchanges.

I've stopped shopping at stores where the cashiers don't say thank you. Think about how rude it is to spend your money in a store, hand the cashier your money, and then all they do is plop the change in your hand and turn to the next person in line.

There's a nationwide drugstore whose name begins with the letter "W" that I stopped going to for that very reason. In multiple exchanges with multiple cashiers, not one of them ever said thank you. It's as if they were specifically trained not to say those very words.

When you thank someone for anything other than a quick exchange, include a detail of what you're thanking them for. Say or write, "Thank you for helping me move," or "Thanks for taking the time to meet with me."

If you're thanking someone for anything major, send them a handwritten thank you card. That used to be a commonplace practice, but today no one does it. If you do it, you'll stand out.

Always send a handwritten thank you card after a job interview and do it within 24 hours. If you don't know the name or address of the person you're interviewing with, ask them for a business card at your interview. When the interview is finished, leave the premises, fill out the card and the envelope you're sending it in, and mail them. (Have your envelope stamped and ready to go in advance.)

Who Says a Man Should Never Apologize?

The words "excuse me" and "I'm sorry" are also very powerful. They can diffuse a potentially ugly situation. I've seen brawls break out and heads busted, because two people bumped into each other and neither one said excuse me.

Not apologizing can also create conflict. When you make a mistake or when you're wrong about something, say so and move on. Only make sure you actually are wrong. You should never apologize out of social pressure or political correctness. If you make a truthful statement and some low-IQ moron is offended by it, that's on them, not you. In modern society, there are people who spend their entire day looking for things to be offended by. Don't apologize to them under any circumstances.

Now there are plenty of dumb, wannabe tough guys who will tell you that a man should never apologize; that it's a sign of weakness. People who say that tend to be overweight slobs who don't know anything about anything. They've spent their entire life drinking beer and watching John Wayne movies and believe that qualifies them to be an expert on life. They're relics of the past. They're also foolish hypocrites.

They're foolish in not recognizing that contrary to being a sign of weakness, apologizing when appropriate is a sign of manners, upbringing, and strength. Admitting when you're wrong and apologizing is tough. It takes a level of courage that most people simply do not have. Perhaps that's why the wannabe tough guys avoid it.

They're also hypocrites. They boast of never apologizing, but when they bump into someone bigger than they are, they slobber all over themselves apologizing.

If you bump into somebody or interrupt them while they're talking, say excuse me or I'm sorry. Those simple words will immediately diffuse the situation.

Here are some other ways to practice politeness.

Don't make fun of people. Watch your jokes in that regard. If you have a good joke, tell it. But never tell a joke or make a remark that hurts someone else's feelings.

Don't tell dirty jokes.

Don't jump lines or cut in front of people.

Don't put your elbows on the table when eating.

Chew your food with your mouth closed and don't talk with food in your mouth. If someone asks you a question while you're eating, finish chewing first and swallow your food down, then answer the question.

Don't flip people off. You probably have some friends who think flipping the bird is funny or a sign of toughness. It's neither. It's stupid and rude. And if you do it to the wrong person, watch out.

Don't curse or use bad language. It's a sign of immaturity that most men never grow out of. The best way not to fall into that trap is to not start doing it in the first place.

Don't ask a woman how old she is. That sounds stupid, I know. But trust me, don't do it.

Don't ask a man how much money he makes. Similar to the above, don't do it. If someone asks you how much money you make, tell them, "Plenty," or "Enough to get by," and let it go at that.

Don't comment or make fun of other people's looks.

Don't gossip or talk about people behind their backs.

If you're out walking with a girl, walk on the outside, closest to the street. If you come to a door, open it and hold it for her. Do that for any female.

Don't cut off other cars in traffic. Doing so can get you killed two ways. First, the other car could slam into yours,

11

killing you in an accident. Second, the driver of the other car could pull out a gun and start blasting. People die in road rage incidents like that all the time.

Don't turn your car around in other people's driveways.

Don't cut across people's yards. The people who own those yards hate it. So would you. It takes a lot of time and money to buy and upkeep a house, and even more time and money to grow a nice-looking lawn. Imagine if you had spent all that money and put all that time into growing a nice lawn and then you look out your window and there's some punk tramping across it.

When I was 13, my buddy and I cut across people's yards all the time. The more we got yelled at, the more we did it. Then one day we were cutting across a yard and a nice woman approached us and said, "Boys, could you please do me a favor? I spend a lot of time working on my yard; could you please not cut across it? I would really appreciate it."

We assured her we wouldn't and we never did again.

That story has two lessons. First, it shows just how much people care about their yards.

Second, it shows the power of the word "please." When people yelled at us to stay off their yards, we didn't listen and kept doing it. But when someone approached us in a nice way and asked us politely not to walk on her lawn, we immediately complied.

Because she respected us, we respected her.

Being polite sometimes means showing respect for traditional customs. Standing for the National Anthem is one such custom. Taking your hat off in church is another. You don't do these things because everyone else is doing them—

that would be conformity. You do them because it's the right thing to do. If no one else stands for the National Anthem or takes their hat off in church, you should still do it.

Being polite basically boils down to doing the right thing at the right time. If you bump into someone, say excuse me. If someone does you a favor, say thank you. If people don't want you cutting across their lawn, don't do it. If you feel an urge to make a smart remark, keep your mouth shut. It's really that simple.

An Ounce of Prevention is Worth a Pound of Cure

It's far easier to prevent trouble from occurring than it is to get out of trouble once you're in it. With that in mind, it's worth noting that people are more apt to be rude when they're in a hurry.

That's when you're likely to see them speeding in traffic and cutting in front of other drivers. That's when people are more likely to snap and make comments that they regret later.

Knowing that, one of the best ways to ensure that *you* won't be rude is to plan ahead, to always leave early for wherever you're going, and to give yourself plenty of time to get there and do what you need to do. Plan your life so you never feel rushed.

The Greek philosopher Aristotle is credited with saying, "We are what we repeatedly do. Excellence then is not an act, but a habit."

Make it your habit to always be polite.

Remember, nobody likes a smartass.

Chapter Two

Tell the Truth, Even When It's Hard

"He who tells the truth gets chased out of nine villages."—old Turkish proverb

People lie.

When I say people, I mean everyone. You might think that people your own age lie a lot, but let me tell you something, people your own age have nothing on adults. Adults lie all the time—about everything.

The biggest liars in the world today work in the news media. Virtually everyone employed in the mainstream news media on any level is a liar. Every newscaster, every reporter, and every radio talk show host in the country is a liar. The ones who deny it the loudest are the ones who lie the most.

Right behind them are teachers, professors, doctors, dentists, nurses, pharmacists, school officials, politicians, lawyers, judges, bankers, book publishers, marketing professionals, and anyone employed in the entertainment industry. They're all liars, and we've only scratched the surface. The world is so full of crooks, liars, and charlatans that I might be the only adult in your life who has ever spoken honestly to you, and this might be the only book you've ever read which dares to tell you the truth.

Not everyone is lying intentionally. Some of them are merely repeating lies that they've been told. But a lie is still a lie, whether it's secondhand or firsthand.

In a world filled with liars, I'm advising you to be different; to do the exact opposite of what everyone else is doing and tell the truth.

If the thought of being different makes you nervous, it shouldn't. Only the individual who dares to be different can rise to heights of awareness and consciousness. The more you belong to the crowd and remain like everyone else, the deeper you fall into darkness.

If you decide to always tell the truth, you will be a rare individual; one in a million, or possibly one in ten million. That's because most people do not seek the truth. Instead they seek what is pleasing to them, or more accurately, what is pleasing to their false view of themselves. Truth makes them squirm so they deny it.

Pursuing the truth is a masculine enterprise. It takes spiritual fortitude. Pursuing the truth will bring you closer to God, because God is truth.

Rejection of the truth and believing in lies will do just the opposite. They will take you away from God.

To believe in lies a person must be emotionally vulnerable, which is a feminine trait. That's why feminized men lie all the time.

The more you pursue the truth and the more truth reveals itself to you, the easier it will be for you to spot obvious lies. You will eventually reach the point where it will be impossible for anyone to lie to you, because you'll spot it right away.

In order to pursue truth, you have to go all-in. You can't say, "I'll take this truth here, but not that truth there." You have to take *all* the truth and let the chips fall where they may. Hardly anyone is willing to do that.

Honesty is the Best Policy

Telling the truth simplifies your life.

One of the reasons why people are so stressed out today is because they can't keep track of all the lies; both the lies they tell and the lies being told to them. When a person lies, they have to remember all of the little details that went into their lie, and then they have to remember the details of all the other lies they told in order to support their original lie. Over time, that's hard to do. That's why people who tell the truth look a lot younger than those who don't.

It takes a lot of energy to hold back the truth. Once you release that energy and allow the truth to flow easily through you, your facial features soften and the years melt away. You can see this in practice with the adults in your life. Don't some of them look young for their age, while others don't?

A person who lies to others must first lie to himself. That's where the damage is done. Lying compromises the immune system. A person who lies is hurting their health and setting themselves up for a life of premature aging.

Look at American presidents both before and after they leave office. A president's term lasts only four years, but almost every man who's held the office looks twenty years older when his term is finished compared to when his term began. That's because they've done nothing but lie their entire time in office.

Barack Obama lied so much during his time in office, his hair turned completely gray. In recent years, only two presidents have looked exactly the same on their last day in office as they did on their first day: Ronald Reagan and Donald Trump. Perhaps they didn't lie as much as the others.

Do This to Make People Trust You

When you tell the truth, people trust you. And because honesty is so rare, that trust opens a lot of doors that might not ordinarily open.

Telling the truth is also good for society. History proves that and the most obvious example is Christian Europe.

When Christianity prevailed in Europe, societies flourished. Music, art, literature, and life in general were all at a high level, far higher than they are today. Magnificent cathedrals were built, children were loved and well treated, marriages were steady and nobody got divorced. It was probably the happiest time in all of history to be alive.

One of the reasons for all of that happiness is because people told the truth. In Christianity, truth is the highest virtue. Even people who oppose Christianity acknowledge that. People in Europe were compelled by their Christian faith to be honest, to speak truth to power, even if it hurt them. Those who were afraid to speak out at least acknowledged the truth within themselves. They didn't lie to themselves and attempt to twist the truth in order to justify their cowardice, as people do today.

When Christianity was removed from Europe, truth was the first thing to go. Everything that was moral, honest, and true became corrupt, dishonest and false. The entire continent fell apart. Today, Europe is a shambles. Sin and perversion are everywhere, crime is rampant, and no one is safe. Life in Europe in the 21st century is a free-for-all and truth is whatever a person decides in the moment.

The same thing is happening right now in America. Christianity is all but extinguished and truth no longer exists. American society has become so fake and so full of lies, the truth actually hurts people.

I mean that literally. The truth causes people to experience actual physical pain to the point where they either run away from it or demand that it be shut down and censored.

When truth reveals something that people don't like, they become hysterical. Take FBI crime statistics which show that black Americans make up only 13% of the population in this country, but commit over 40% of the violent crime, including 50% of the murders and 60% of the rapes. When people hear those numbers they shriek like little girls and cover their ears. The truth actually hurts them. Some people reading this—feminized men and mentally ill women—are experiencing pain right now.

Because so many people are hurt by the truth, we're no longer supposed to speak truthfully. We're supposed to lie in order not to "offend" people. When confronted with an uncomfortable truth, such as FBI crime statistics, society as a whole is expected to close their eyes and pretend those numbers don't exist, or to attack whoever it was that brought them up in the first place. The one thing we're not allowed to do, the only sensible response really, is to ask why those numbers are so high and what we can do to bring them down. But you see that's not allowed.

The person who asks why those numbers are so high and what we can do to bring them down is actively seeking the truth. The person who says we can't talk about those numbers and pretends they don't exist is running away from the truth. Big difference.

Not only that, but when crimes are committed by black Americans, and those crimes take place hundreds of times a day all across the country, we're supposed to act like we're surprised and we have no idea why it's happening. Or worse, we're supposed to say it's because of white people.

That's how far gone from reality we are.

America is an Open Air Insane Asylum

How far removed from reality are we, you ask? Pretty far. We're as far removed from reality as you could possibly imagine. No, wait. I take that back. We're even farther removed from reality than you could possibly imagine. Much, much farther.

Former CIA director William Casey famously said, "We'll know our disinformation program is complete when everything the American people believe is false."

We're at that point now. Virtually everything the American people believe is a lie. They have been duped into believing the most ridiculous absurdities, and no amount of facts, evidence, or downright proof is going to change their minds. They're hopelessly brainwashed, hopelessly lost, and so far removed from reality that they don't even know what reality is anymore.

Perhaps you're wondering if there's a way you can help these people and bring them back to the truth. I used to wonder about that myself. If the person you're hoping to help is young, or at least young at heart, you might have a chance to save them. But for anyone else, forget it. There's simply no possibility of helping people who are so dishonest and so delusional in their thinking that they can't see what's in front of their own nose. Sin dulls the senses and most people are so mired in sin that they are never coming back to reality. At least not until they die and find themselves in hell. They'll get a dose of reality then.

Take the case of tranny mania that's currently sweeping the country. Fat, dumb Americans are so beyond hope that they're now willfully accepting the ultimate evil: the sexual mutilation of children.

Think of it: millions of Americans stuffing their face with pizza, watching television, and jerking off to pornography, while thousands of innocent little children are being groomed and indoctrinated into homosexuality by their own parents and school teachers. Can it get any worse than that?

The Bible is hundreds of pages long—hundreds of pages of exceedingly small print—yet among all of those words and pages there are only four sins that the Bible says cry out to

Heaven for vengeance. One of those four sins is homosexuality.

Early on in the Bible is the story of Sodom and Gomorrah. The inhabitants of those two cities were practicing rampant homosexuality. As punishment for their sins, God rained down sulfur and fire, utterly destroying both cities and everyone in them. He nuked both cities.

Modern day archaeologists have discovered the charred and ruined remains of Sodom and Gomorrah. Those cities actually existed. And the reason why God choose fire and brimstone to destroy them rather than other means was to serve as a stark reminder to humanity that anyone who engages in homosexuality is going to end up burning for eternity in the fires of hell. That's pretty intense.

What the Bible Says about Trannyism

The Bible also addresses cross-dressing and trannyism. Yes, it was going on back then. The Bible says, "The woman shall not wear that which pertaineth unto a man, neither shall a man put on a woman's garment: for all that do so are abomination unto the Lord thy God." (Deut 22:5)

So God and the Bible condemn cross-dressing and call it an abomination. But trannyism isn't just wearing the clothes of the opposite sex. It's far worse than that. In the United States today, thousands of children every year are having their bodies mutilated in a sick attempt to alter their God-given gender.

What that sick attempt to alter their gender entails is going to sound absolutely disgusting, but in order to understand what's happening you need to know the truth. If you have a queasy stomach, you may want to skip the next paragraph or even flip to the next page. I think you're man enough to take what I'm about to say, but I don't want you to faint. When I was your age and first heard about the horrible ways that Christians were persecuted, tortured, and murdered, it made me want to vomit. If you think you might be like that, flip to the next page. For those willing to face the truth, keep reading.

First, in order to change a child's gender, they are given sex hormones. Little boys are given female sex hormones, and little girls are given male sex hormones. Those sex hormones block the child's natural development—the development that God intended. After that comes the real gruesome part. The boys have their penises chopped off and the girls have their breasts chopped off.

Like I said, totally sick and disgusting. And not only is it legal, it's supported and encouraged by the entire United States government, the entire United States military, the entire mainstream media, every airline in the country, every professional sports league in the country, every facet of the entertainment industry—movies, television, music, and books, and every corporation and school in the country.

Did you catch that last part? Trannyism is being promoted and pushed by teachers in every school in the country, including *your* school. According to the New York Post, there are over 168 school districts nationwide, comprised of over 6,000 schools, and serving over 3 million students, that have rules in place that prevent faculty and staff from disclosing to parents a student's "gender status."

In other words, there are thousands of sick and twisted teachers in schools all across the country working around the clock to groom and indoctrinate children into homosexuality and trannyism, and they have enacted rules to prevent anyone else at their school from disclosing that information to the parents of the children they are grooming. It's all being done in secret.

Corrupt politicians in the state of Washington just passed a bill that makes it legal for children to be kidnapped from their parents, taken to a secret "youth shelter," and forcibly "transitioned" to the opposite sex. (Senate Bill 5599)

The people pushing trannyism, including your teachers, are the sickest, most perverted scumbags to ever live. They're sick beyond belief and every one of them is mentally ill.

In a sane society, confused kids would receive guidance and counseling, and the adults forcing them into trannyism and homosexuality would be locked up for life, including the brain-dead parents who allow their children to be sexually mutilated. None of those adults would be allowed within a mile of a child. None of them would be allowed to even walk the street.

But we don't live in a sane society.

We live in an open air insane asylum.

Trannyism is Satanism

The Bible speaks of harming children. Jesus says, "And whosoever shall offend one of these little ones that believe in me, it is better for him that a millstone were hanged about his neck, and he were cast into the sea." (Mark 9:42)

That's one of the harshest declarations in the Bible. It ranks right up there with God's use of fire and brimstone to punish homosexuality. Now combine homosexuality with the grooming and sexual mutilation of children that's currently being carried out all across the country. The people behind that disgusting agenda are committing two of the worst sins imaginable—homosexuality and the harming of children.

Can you imagine the unspeakable horror and eternal suffering that awaits them when they die and go to hell? I shudder to think about it. But wait, it gets even worse. Trannyism is actually Satanism.

The universal symbol of Satanism is Baphomet, a half-human, half-goat creation. In fact, Baphomet is actually used to depict Satan himself. When you see a picture of Baphomet, you are seeing a picture of Satan.

Baphomet is half male and half female. In other words, Baphomet is a tranny and the use of Baphomet to represent Satanism is telling the entire world in clear, unmistakable language that trannyism is Satanism.

Can you see just how sick and perverted this world is?

The people pushing trannyism say that children as young as 3, 4, and 5 have the mental capacity to decide they want their bodies to be permanently and sexually mutilated.

Children that age have no idea what they're doing. They can't even tie their own shoe, but adult groomers tell us that they are old enough to decide they want a permanent sex change operation.

A person has to be literally insane to believe that. Yet that's the official position of our government, our military, and our media, along with every airline, every professional sports league, every branch of the entertainment industry, and every major corporation and school in the country.

These people are sick—sick in the head and sick in the soul. They are acting on impulses from the deepest, darkest pits of hell. That's where they're going when they die and they want to drag as many people down to hell with them as they can. Are you on their team?

If you didn't just shout, "Hell no!" as loud as you can, you need to put this book down and do 100 pushups.

To show you just how widespread this sickness is, in 2007, there were two pediatric (children's) "gender clinics" in the United States. Today there are almost 200. These "gender clinics" are where innocent little children are taken by their sick parents and perverted school officials to be given hormone pills and have their sex organs chopped off.

Do the math. If 200 pediatric "gender clinics" are each "transitioning" 100 kids a year (and that's a conservative estimate, it's only 8 kids a month, not enough to keep these "clinics" open), it equals 20,000 kids a year, and 200,000 kids every ten years. Literally tens of thousands of innocent little children are getting sexually molested and mutilated by these freaks, yet where's the outrage? Who else besides me is even telling you about this?

By the way, almost everyone in the country today is actively supporting trannyism, whether they know it or not.

If someone works for the federal government, they're supporting trannyism for the simple reason that the government supports trannyism.

Sure, they might not agree with the government's position on trannyism, but as long as they remain employed by the government they're still a cog in the wheel. And that makes them responsible.

If someone enlists in the military, they're supporting trannyism, because the military supports trannyism. If someone flies, they're supporting trannyism, because every airline in the country supports trannyism. If someone watches a sporting event, they're supporting trannyism, because every professional sports league in the country supports trannyism.

Even the simple act of watching television, going to a movie, or buying a product made by a major corporation makes one complicit in the sin of trannyism, because that person's money is going to the very people pushing trannyism the hardest.

This is an extremely important point, yet it goes in one ear and out the other of everyone who should know better.

"Divine scripture testifies that an equal punishment is due to those who commit an evil and to those who assent to it."—Pope St. Gregory VII, 1075

A Nation of Liars and Cowards

This is where cowardice rears its ugly head. A lot of people have some idea of what's going on, not only with the sexual mutilation and forced trannyism of innocent children, but with everything else that's wrong with the world today.

Even simple-minded people can tell the world is out of whack. Yet they claim there's nothing they can do about it. When people say this, when they throw up their hands and claim they don't know what to do, they're rarely telling the truth. They know exactly what to do, but they're too cowardly to do it.

In many cases, the appropriate response for them would be to leave their place of employment and work for someone who's not promoting homosexuality and trannyism. For others, the appropriate response is to immediately stop flying, immediately stop watching television, immediately stop following professional sports, immediately stop buying products from major corporations, and so on.

See how easy those solutions are? Yet, how many people do you know who actually have the courage to follow through on them? I'm guessing the answer is zero.

People are frightened of leaving their jobs, because they're too weak and too lazy to find something better. They won't stop flying, watching sports, or buying products made by evil corporations, because they're too weak and too pathetic to give up their addiction to sports, gambling, and visiting Las Vegas. They're too feeble to give up their addiction to decadent vacations, shopping and wasting their money on clothes, cosmetics, electronic gadgets, and junk.

You could make a case that the most destructive behavior in the world today isn't evil itself, but the enabling of evil by Americans who continue to fly, continue to follow professional sports, and continue to provide financial support to the very companies, organizations, and corporations that push evil the hardest.

If you're attending a school that accepts trannyism on any level, guess what? You're guilty of the same sin. Are you going to fold like a cheap tent and go along with it, or are you going to be a man and say no? There's no middle ground in this fight. You're either with God or you're not.

If some blue-haired Communist teacher tries to make you call a boy at your school by a girl's name, or call a girl at your school by a boy's name, tell her no, and refuse to do it.

If that same teacher tries to convince you that trannyism is anything other than a sick and perverted sin before God, tell her to shove it. And then stand your ground. Don't back down under any circumstances.

You might have to stand alone. Your classmates might be so brainwashed by this point and so cowardly that they won't come to your defense. But are you going to stand with God, or with the Satanist scum who get their jollies by molesting and mutilating children?

If your school plays hardball and threatens to suspend or expel you, tell them you'll get a lawyer and sue the crap out of them. Let them know that if they try to force you to go against your religious beliefs, you'll sue each of them personally in addition to suing the school. That will shut them up. Only talk to your parents first, before the situation escalates to that point.

If your parents support this insane tranny agenda, you've really got your work cut out for you. Talk to your dad first. It's impossible for any adult male who isn't homosexual or completely feminized to support the sexual mutilation of children. Explain to him what's going on. Many people still don't understand what's at stake or what they're dealing with. They think trannyism is a fad kids go through, like dressing up for Halloween. If your parents belong to that camp, you're going to have to educate them.

Can you see now why truth is so lacking in society? Standing for truth requires courage; courage that very few people have. The majority of men today are weaklings and cowards, and women are even worse. You'll get little to no support from either of them.

Don't have anything to do with the tranny freaks at your school or the homosexual teachers who encourage them. Don't talk to them. Don't sit or walk near them. Don't participate in sports with them. Treat them like lepers and cut them out of your life completely.

Do that with any sinful person in your life. They've chosen to spend eternity in hell, so let them. Cut them out of your life and don't look back. Failure to do so puts your own soul at risk of eternal damnation. And if you do get suspended or expelled from school, consider it a blessing.

Are Lies Ever Justified?

Telling the truth doesn't mean being rude, although it sometimes means stating facts that other people don't want to hear. Common sense should dictate to you when it's right to speak up and when it's best to keep quiet.

There's also the issue of lying in order to prevent a greater evil. After the Communist takeover of Russia in 1917, tens of millions of Christians were rounded up, brutally tortured, and murdered. If you were living in Russia at the time, with a Christian family hiding in your attic, and a gang of gun-toting commie pukes showed up at your door, wanting to know if you knew where that Christian family was, it would not be a sin to lie and say no.

By telling such a small lie, you would be preventing a much greater evil: the torture and murder of that Christian family. That's a common sense call.

Now there will be times in your life when people will think you're lying even when you're telling the truth. That's because most people (virtually all adults) hear what they want to hear, not what is actually being said. You could say, "The sky is blue," and they'll swear up and down you said, "The sky is green."

In a situation like that, the issue lies not with you, but with them. You're responsible for what you say, not for what others think you say.

Are You That Way?

We've spoken quite a bit about homosexuality and trannyism in this chapter. Before moving on, let's examine one aspect we haven't covered. What if you're a guy who thinks he likes guys? Or worse, a guy who thinks he's a girl?

First, I'd advise you to make sure that's how you really feel and not some nonsense pumped into your head by a child-molesting teacher.

Second, I'd say don't wear women's clothes and don't engage in any type of homosexual behavior under any circumstances. Doing so will send you straight to hell. You'll just have to stay celibate. We all have crosses to bear and that will be yours. Don't whine and say that it's too hard. Your situation is no different from that of thousands of Incels—men who like girls, but who can't get a date—or from guys who *can* get a date, but choose not to.

My neighborhood is swarming with cute girls. When the weather is warm, which it is nine months out of every year, they run around half-naked. That's a lot of temptation. But I abstain from it, because sex outside of marriage is a sin, and also because I don't want to deal with the constant drama and effort it takes to fool around with a girl whose intellect happens to be miles below mine.

Sure, I'd like the thrill of indulging—and could if I wanted to—but it's just not worth it to me at this point.

The third thing I would say to anyone reading this who thinks (falsely) that he's homosexual, is to immediately begin praying and to immediately embrace the traditional Catholic Faith. Doing so will get you through any temptation you feel and alleviate your stress from abstaining. It will put you on a trajectory to Heaven.

Follow the Advice of Jacinta from Fatima

Like everything else, living a totally truthful life is simple, but not easy. The best way to proceed is to follow the advice of little Jacinta of Fatima when she said, "Always tell the truth, even when it is hard."

Jacinta was one of three seers at Fatima, where the Miracle of the Sun took place. The Miracle of the Sun is known as one of the greatest miracles in the history of the world, certainly the greatest miracle since the Resurrection. To learn more about Fatima and the Miracle of the Sun, and I suggest you do, read the book *Our Lady of Fatima* by William Thomas Walsh, one of the most beautiful books you will ever read.

For many people, the most difficult part of living a totally truthful life is admitting that they lie. So they won't do it. Instead, they continue to lie by claiming they live an honest life. Let's see just how honest they are.

Charging too much for a product, service, or housing is a form of lying. People who are guilty of such a lie will draw themselves up and claim that's not true. They'll say they are merely charging "what they are worth" or "fair market value." But that is just another lie.

Paying employees as cheaply as possible is a form of lying. Again, many will protest. But they are only lying to themselves.

False or misleading advertising is a form of lying.

Pushing drugs, fake vaccines, and unnecessary surgery and calling yourself a doctor is a form of lying, the worst and most treacherous form of lying.

Teaching fake history in a classroom is a form of lying.

Manufacturing and selling processed food, which isn't really food at all, is a form of lying.

And on it goes . . . Practically every occupation in the world today requires a person to lie on some level.

Truth is easy to verify. All it takes is a little research, but most people are too stupid and too lazy to do that. It's easier for them to believe lies coming from the mouths of known liars, than it is to pick up a book or visit a website.

There is no escaping the truth. There's no escaping God's law. A person is either telling the truth or they are lying. There is no middle ground. There is no relative truth.

Each of us has an obligation, a duty, to learn the truth and to expose falsehoods and lies. Those who ignore reality, who turn their nose up at facts and truthful evidence, because reality, facts and truthful evidence make them uncomfortable, are doing a tremendous disservice to themselves and to society.

When a delusional person rejects reality, they need others to play along with them, to also reject reality. Otherwise, their world will stop making sense. They'll be forced to admit that their entire life is a lie. That's why a delusional person will become angry when others don't conform to their false view of reality. That's why a man wearing a dress will insist that you call him by a woman's name and become angry when you don't. He needs you to confirm his false reality.

Because cowardice is the fallback position for most Americans, they will go along with what they know are lies, rather than risk criticism for insisting on truth. Don't be that way yourself. Insist on truth.

At the same time, do it intelligently. If you post anything on social media that's true or honest, the freaks living in fantasy land will try to get you kicked out of school or fired from your job.

In current time America, the defining difference between being a man vs. being a feminized male is the desire to seek the truth and the mental capacity to process it. It's also the difference between going to Heaven or hell. There's a direct connection between believing lies and embracing sin.

Being polite is your first step on the road to manhood.

Your second step is to seek the truth and always tell the truth, even when it's hard. To stand up for truth and not to participate in lies no matter what the cost.

Chapter Three

Kill Your Television

"Television, the drug of the nation
"Breeding ignorance and feeding radiation."
—Disposable Heroes of Hiphoprisy

Everything you see on television is a lie.

I'm not exaggerating when I say that. Literally everything you've ever seen on television (or heard on the radio) since the day you were born is a lie. Let's look at a couple of recent examples that you can easily verify for yourself.

Everything you saw on television regarding the 2020 presidential election is a lie. Donald Trump won the 2020 election by a wide margin, but because he won, and because he won so decisively, the "voting" in several key states was suspended until the corrupt election officials in those states could create enough fake ballots in the middle of the night to make it look like he didn't win. Then they boarded up the windows so no one could see them counting the fake ballots.

The well-paid liars on television immediately told us that this massive fraud we were witnessing was how "democracy" works, and that Sleepy Joe, who couldn't draw more than forty people to a rally, somehow finished with the most votes of anyone in history. A person has to be literally retarded to believe that.

Yet many people do believe it, and they happen to be the same perverts and sickos who believe that children as young as three have the mental capacity to demand a permanent sex change operation. These sickos and perverts are the only people in the country who legitimately voted for Sleepy Joe. Everyone who's not a sicko or pervert voted for Trump.

Anyone who tells you that Hair-Sniffing Joe won the 2020 presidential election is either deliberately lying or so fundamentally stupid they should never be listened to again.

Let's look at another example of television lying to you that you can easily verify for yourself.

Everything you saw on television regarding the "pandemic" of 2020-2022 is a lie.

Wait, you mean you thought it was all real?

I've written four books on the fake pandemic. If you want to know how millions of mush-brained morons around the world were duped into believing that a non-existent virus was a real thing, you can find all of the sordid details in those books. I'll give you a few choice tidbits here to get you started.

For starters, there wasn't even a real virus; the Canadian government admitted that in court.

A man named Patrick King, a private citizen in Alberta, Canada represented himself in court after being fined $1,200 for protesting his province's lockdowns. King subpoenaed the Provincial Health Minister, Dr. Deena Hinshaw, for proof that the COVID-19 virus actually existed. Guess what happened?

The Health Minister admitted in court that they had no evidence that the virus actually exists because it has never been isolated. The Province was then forced to rescind all of their COVID restrictions, because they had no legal standing to enforce them over a nonexistent virus. Did you hear about that in school?

The CDC (Center for Disease Control) also admitted that the COVID-19 virus does not exist.

In one of their own documents from July of 2020 entitled "CDC 2019-Novel Coronavirus (2019-nCoV) Real-Time RT-PCR Diagnostic Panel", they wrote on page 39, "Since no quantified virus isolates of the 2019-nCoV are currently available, assays [diagnostic tests] designed for detection of the 2019-nCoV RNA were tested with characterized stocks of in vitro transcribed full length RNA."

What that psycho-babble basically says is the same thing the Canadian government admitted in court: the virus has never been isolated.

Read the very beginning of the CDC's admission again: "Since no quantified virus isolates of the 2019-nCoV are currently available . . ."

There it is—no virus isolates are available. If you can't isolate a virus, then it doesn't exist. Both the Canadian government and the CDC admit this.

Did you know that a coronavirus is nothing more than a cold virus? You can research that yourself by consulting a virology textbook. The COVID-19 "virus" which doesn't exist is nothing more than a renaming of the common cold.

Did you know that not one person in the entire world actually died from what we were told was the COVID-19 virus? People died from cancer, heart attacks, the fake vaccine, being hooked up to ventilators, motorcycle accidents, and falling off ladders and their deaths were *attributed* to COVID-19, but not one person actually died *from* COVID-19.

How could they when it doesn't exist?

Did you know that the death rate for the United States was no higher in 2020 when the "pandemic" was supposedly raging than it has been for the last five years?

Did you know that a former FDA Commissioner admitted that the six-foot social distancing rule was completely made up and that nobody knows where it came from?

Did you know that the Norwegian Institute of Public Health declared COVID-19 to be no worse than the flu?

Did you know that Secretary of State Mike Pompeo when speaking of the "pandemic" in March of 2020 said, "We're in a live exercise here."

A live exercise is not a real event. With those words, Pompeo admitted that the whole thing was a drill, not an actual event.

I could go one for hundreds of pages, but you get the idea. If you want to know more about the fake pandemic, you can check out my other books. What's important for you to realize now is that the whole thing was a farce and its purpose was to trick people into taking a fake vaccine. To date, over 4 million people worldwide have died from the fake vaccine and millions more have been crippled and injured. None of that would have been possible without the use of television to brainwash the masses.

The question to ask then is if television lied to us about the fraudulent 2020 presidential election . . . if they lied to us about the fake pandemic . . . then what else have they lied to us about?

The answer is everything.

In fact, if you want to know what the truth is about any given subject, the easiest way to do that is to know that the truth is the exact opposite of whatever is being reported on television. Whatever television tells you is true, is actually a lie; and whatever they say is a lie, is actually true.

If television tells you that something or someone is a "threat to Democracy" and does not represent "who we are as Americans," you can bet your bottom dollar that whatever or whoever they are denouncing is absolutely fabulous for the country and exactly who we are as Americans.

If television tells you that someone is a hero whose name and life deserve to be celebrated, know that whoever they are praising is a piece of Communist scum that deserves to be hung from the highest lamp post.

Anytime you see something being promoted as good on television that means it's bad. And anytime you see something being called bad on television that means it's good.

Television does its dirty work by taking something sick and calling it normal. Then they glamourize it, help to legalize it, and present it as something desirable.

If you find yourself agreeing with anything being promoted on television, you need to stop and reconsider your position. You're letting emotionalism (a feminine trait) cloud your judgment.

Television is rotting your brain with all of its lies and hypnotic programming. It's setting you up for failure. Television is telling you to hate what's good and love what's bad. It's telling you to hate your race. It's telling you to hate yourself.

Television represents everything that is wrong with the world today. It ridicules the family, fatherhood, and Christianity—the three virtues most lacking in society today, while simultaneously promoting abortion, homosexuality, trannyism, race-mixing, criminal behavior, rampant drug use, endless wars, the sexualizing of children, and more. That is television's purpose, to brainwash the masses by denouncing everything good and promoting everything bad.

If you're surprised by any of this, you shouldn't be. We talked in the last chapter about how almost every adult in your life is lying to you. Television is merely an extension of that.

Between your teachers at school and the television in your living room, you're being bombarded with lies every hour of every day. Somebody has to stand up and tell you the truth, so it may as well be me.

Television Dumbs People Down

There are decades worth of studies, too numerous to count, that all come to the same conclusion: people who watch television on any given subject know far less about that same subject than people who don't watch television. For instance, people who watch television news know less about what's being reported on the news than people who don't watch television. Television dumbs people down.

Take It from an Insider

I've worked in television and movies. I know exactly what they are doing. It's not about entertainment. It's not even about money, although money plays a part. What television, movies, and music are about is turning society upside down by making the abnormal appear normal. And they've been doing it successfully for a very long time. It's a sick and twisted agenda and it drives them relentlessly.

The people who work in television hold you, the viewer, in utter contempt. To them you are literally human scum. If I told you the giddy delight the people who work in television take in mocking you with fake news, woke programming, and insulting sitcoms, you would never watch television again. That is, if you have self-esteem. If not, you'll keep watching.

Television Is a Drug

A drug is a substance which has a physiological or psychological effect when introduced into the body. As a verb, the word "drug" describes the process of administering something to someone in order to induce a stupor or insensibility, such as: *he was drugged to keep him quiet.*

Television meets both definitions.

Like all drugs, television creates addicts. You might be one of them. Can you stop watching television? Can you stop right now? How about for the next two weeks? The next three weeks? If not, you're an addict. You're no different than a junkie shooting up in the street, only your drug of choice isn't heroin, it's television.

Millions of people are addicted to television.

They alter their daily routine in order not to miss their favorite shows. They rush home from work so they can sit like zombies in front of a screen. They engage in heated discussion and debates over purely fictional characters that populate television and film. They are television addicts.

The people who work in television know they have the old folks hooked, so now they're after the young ones and especially children.

All children's programming on television today is filled with sick and twisted sexual references in order to groom them into having sex with homosexual men and women. If you have younger brothers or sisters, they're being targeted by these perverts whenever they watch television.

Television encourages (brainwashes) women to become more masculine, and men to become more feminine. It does this by convincing women to abandon their traditional role as wives and mothers in favor of the more masculine pursuit of a career.

When was the last time you saw a woman on television being celebrated for being a good wife or mother?

Probably never. Meanwhile, how many times have you seen women on television celebrated for being liars, whores, and manipulators, obsessed with sex and acting like fools?

Every hour of every day.

Television brainwashes men into abandoning their traditional role as providers and protectors of society, and accepting and embracing all manner of deviant behavior, including feminism, homosexuality, and trannyism.

When was the last time you saw a man on television being celebrated for being a good husband or father?

You will never see a man portrayed that way on modern television.

Sportsball is for Simps and Suckers

Perhaps the most pathetic of all television watchers are men who watch sports. Not only is it a colossal waste of time, but the sports leagues they're addicted to watching—football, baseball, basketball, and hockey—are all open supporters of homosexuality and trannyism (the sexual mutilation of children).

All of these leagues sponsor Pride Nights. They all encourage their players to wear pink jerseys and cleats. They all came out in support of looting and lawlessness, during the riots of 2019-20. They all came out in support of the fake pandemic of 2020-22.

In other words, all of the major sports leagues promote sin, crime, and the sexual mutilation of children. They all promote feminism and the feminization of men. They all promote everything that God is against.

Yet millions of fat, dumb Americans continue to support these leagues and watch their games. You might find that hard to believe, but fat, dumb Americans are just that—fat and dumb, and they continue to support a product whose owners openly despise them.

Even worse, television encourages feminized men to develop homoerotic "man-crushes" on athletes and actors. Some of these feminized men are so pathetic that they actually buy the jerseys of their favorite sports players and wear them.

You know where that habit comes from—men wearing the jersey of their favorite player? It comes from high school football, where a girl will sometimes wear the jersey of a boy she's dating.

When a feminized man wears the jersey of a professional player, it's no different. He's telling the world that he has a "crush" on that particular person. To put it bluntly, a feminized man wearing the sports jersey of his favorite player is telling the world that he's that player's bitch.

Now if you're in high school or someone under the age of 25 who has grown up idolizing sports stars, you're excused. And don't make fun of any kids you see wearing jerseys either. Like you, they've been lied to by the adults in their life and led to believe that having "heroes" is a healthy thing. I'm telling you it's not. I want you to be your own hero.

As a child must one day put away its toys, you need to stop wearing professional sports jerseys and stop watching the games. Every dollar spent on a jersey or attending a game is a dollar into the pocket of the very people who get off on sexually mutilating children.

It's Even Worse for Girls

Modern society is a funnel to hell and television points the way. Television's negative influence is even worse for girls than it is for boys. You think you have it bad? Look at the brainwashing that young girls are subjected to.

Television targets young girls and encourages them to dress immodestly. Girls see women on television dressed like hookers and receiving positive attention, so they imitate them. They think it's normal, because the media acts like its normal. When no one in their life tells them differently, they continue to do it.

Anytime you see a girl showing her legs, her midriff, or any area of her body, you're looking at a girl who's never had any guidance or honest advice in her life. You're looking at a girl with uncaring, brain-dead parents. You're looking at a girl under the influence of television.

But it doesn't stop there. Television teaches girls that sexual appeal—not beauty, but sexual appeal—is all that matters. It encourages them to abandon their morals and religious beliefs and to engage in every type of sexual perversion imaginable, including homosexuality and trannyism.

Television encourages girls to hate men of their own race, while simultaneously engaging in as much sex as they can with men of other races. Then it encourages them to abort and murder their babies.

If you're a girl reading this, then it's important for you to understand exactly what you're dealing with. You live in a society that attacks your purity in a thousand different ways through movies, music, television, magazines, advertising, and fashion. It's all in your face. Society wants to ensnare you in its satanic grasp and drag your soul to hell. Don't let that happen.

One of the best things you could possibly do is to make a vow to God and to yourself that you will never dress immodestly again. And then keep that vow.

You won't attract as much attention from boys, but that's not a bad thing. By dressing modestly, you'll eliminate a lot of losers from your life. The boys you do attract will be of higher quality and treat you more respectfully. It's a win-win situation.

"How many young girls there are who see nothing wrong in following certain shameless styles like so many sheep. They would certainly blush with shame if they could know the impression they make, and the feelings they evoke, in those who see them."—Pope Pius XII, 1954

The Occult Origins of Television

Are you aware that every time you watch a television show, movie, or streaming service, your mind is being manipulated by an unseen hand?

Have you ever stopped to consider the tremendous influence you are under every time you watch television and allow yourself to be seduced by the hypnotist in the corner?

Do you know why television is even called "television," or why it consists of "programs" and "channels"? Would you be surprised to learn those three words—television, program, and channel—were chosen for their occult connection?

Take the word "television" and break it down. You get *tel-lie-vision*. It means to tell a lie visually.

The word "channel" comes from channeling, a word used by mystics and psychics. Channeling is the process they use to draw in spirits and entities from another world or dimension. Someone who channels a spirit allows that particular entity to access their body and mind, and even to speak through their mouth.

Don't laugh. The process of channeling is huge in witchcraft and the New Age. And the use of the word "channel" as it applies to television is not a coincidence. What we call television channels could have been called stations. That's what they're called in radio. You tune in to a radio station, don't you? Why is the word "channel" used in television? Could it be because television is a black mirror?

Television, computers, and smart phones have long been known in the occult world as "black mirrors." A black mirror is a portal into another world or dimension. Those portals allow spirits to enter into the mortal, material world. In other words, they act as channels.

A British pop band called The Police made an entire album about this called *Ghost in the Machine*. The cover art for that album features a hidden 666 message when viewed in a mirror. The album has songs about demons and sorcery ("Spirits in a Material World"), transhumanism ("Rehumanize Yourself"), and one world government ("One World, Not Three"). The album was made in 1981, before anyone had even heard of a personal computer or iPhone.

The word "channel" was chosen for television, because it more accurately describes what happens when viewers tune in. Television viewers are literally channeling unseen energy and influence into their life.

Why does television describe its content as "programs"?

The word "program" is used in hypnosis, brainwashing, and the occult. To program someone, means to hypnotize or brainwash them. When that process is complete and a person is successfully hypnotized or brainwashed, they are said to be programmed.

Add those three words together—television, channel, and program, and what do you get? You get television viewers being *told lies visually*. You get viewers being *programmed*, and receiving their programming via a *channel(er)*.

Does that sound like a healthy way to spend your time?

Television exists to put people into a trancelike state and then program their mind with repetitive propaganda.

Remember the words of former CIA director William Casey: "We'll know our disinformation program is complete when everything the American people believe is false."

Notice how he used the word program. The CIA through the use of television is programming people's minds.

Do you know what else William Casey bragged about? He claimed that the CIA had every person of any importance in the media under their thumb and on their payroll. In other words, every newscaster, every television personality, every radio talk show host, and every actor or actress you can name has been bought off by the CIA to help promote a Communist agenda. They're all bitches of the CIA.

Purge All Pornography

While we're on the subject of television, this is a good time to point out the need to purge all pornography from your life. If you're not currently reading or watching pornography, you're a good man. Don't ever start.

If you *are* currently reading or watching pornography, it's important to stop immediately and purge it all from your life. There are multiple reasons for doing so.

Pornography has no place in the life of man. It's sinful, it's disgusting, and it leads to masturbation, a mortal sin that will send you straight to hell.

Not only that, but reading or watching pornography is a mortal sin in itself; one that will send you straight to hell. Is the sight of some ugly whore's naked body worth going to hell for?

Women who allow themselves to seen naked or in any form of revealing attire (bathing suits, bikinis, short skirts, etc.) are a blight on humanity and guilty of serious sin. They are literal human scum.

For the thrill of male attention, they're condemning their souls to hell. If you knew them in real life, you'd be appalled and disgusted just being around them. Why in the world would you put your soul in danger of going to hell just to ogle one of these filthy whores?

You may not know this, but one of the main purposes of pornography is the destruction of Christianity. That's why it's so rampant in our society. Al Goldstein, a major producer of pornography, was asked why he did it. Goldstein answered, "The only reason why Jews are in pornography is that we think Christ sucks. Catholicism sucks. Pornography thus becomes a way of defiling Christian culture."

In Goldstein's own words, you can see that the people pushing pornography do it because they hate God. That also applies to the whores who appear in pornography and to everyone that supports it on any level. That includes you if you read or watch pornography.

Can you imagine the immense sorrow you cause Jesus to suffer every time you read or watch pornography? Jesus died on the cross for you . . . you can't stop reading and watching pornography for Him?

If you feel yourself overrun with sexual desire, calm down. You wouldn't feel sexual desire if your grandmother was in the room, so picture her standing there next to you.

If you're burning with lust and temptation, the solution is to pray more. A lot more. Saint Bruno said, "He hath a demon within him who persists in any grave sin."

If that's the case with you, it's going to take some heavy-duty prayer to purge those demons. Praying the Rosary is one of the best ways to do that, and to develop the strength of will to overcome temptation. I can personally vouch for that. So can many others.

Purging yourself of pornography means giving up all dating sites, all hookup sites, and every website where useless whores parade their bodies in exchange for money from feminized men—the biggest purveyors of pornography.

That feminized men are the biggest purveyors of pornography shouldn't surprise you. Feminized men are weak and unable to exert even the slightest bit of willpower when it comes to women and pornography. Feminized men also display symptoms of homosexuality and all pornography is homosexual in nature.

Many men use pornography less as a substitute for sex than they do as a drug. They're addicted to it and can't stop. To them, pornography is an extreme and very destructive way of escaping from reality.

When you make the decision to purge yourself of pornography, and it's a decision you must make, be ready to suffer in the same way that anyone quitting an addiction suffers. The first step is to ask God for help.

Purge yourself of pornography one day at a time. One hour at a time, if that's what it takes. Complete a stretch of eight hours, then sixteen hours, then a full day. When the sun rises in the morning, begin again.

Pornography is a weapon meant to disrupt the family unit and destabilize society. Did you know that? It's yet another purpose of pornography and another reason why it's allowed to flourish as it does. In any sane society, pornography would be outlawed and those who push it would be rounded up and tossed in the slammer. But we don't live in a sane society.

If your buddies encourage you to watch pornography, either with them or by yourself, tell them no and walk away. Then start looking for new friends.

Avoid pointless interactions and flirty banter with women. All that does is lead to an urge for pornography.

Another reason why you need to purge pornography from your life is because the people who produce it are the same lowlife sleazebags who are pushing trannyism and homosexual sex with children. They're homosexuals themselves. They know that anyone who reads or watches pornography will eventually get turned on by homosexuality and want to engage in it. How could they not? And once a person engages in homosexuality, the next step is homosexual sex with children. Thus, by pushing pornography, they are pushing trannyism and the sexual mutilation of children.

Reading or watching pornography will ruin your relationships with women. Romantic relationships are hard enough, as is. Add pornography to the mix and you've just made it ten times harder. I sometimes wonder if the reason why so many men complain of not being able to engage in romance with women is because they read or watch pornography.

If you're a girl reading this, you're just as guilty. The pornography you're consuming, along with your romance novels and celebrity gossip magazines are ruining your relationships with men.

Pornography takes all of the romance out of sex and reduces it to an animal act, devoid of feeling and emotional attachment. It turns humans into animals.

The final reason why you need to purge all pornography from your life is because every dollar you spend on pornography is another dollar into the pockets of those who hate God, hate Christianity, and want to see you dead. They literally want to see you dead. If you continue to read or watch pornography, it makes you an enemy collaborator and a traitor to God.

Two Versions of Reality

Both this chapter and the preceding one have shown you how two completely different versions of reality exist. The first version of reality is determined by facts, evidence, and physical proof. Less than 5% of the American people live in this first version of reality.

The second version of reality is where 95% of the American people live. It's a reality fueled by lies, lunacy, and literal insanity. This is the reality presented to you on television.

It's also the reality occupied by most of your teachers at school, and by practically every adult in your life.

Some people call this second reality Clown World, which is an apt description. Whatever you call it, this second version of reality is a dangerous place that you do not want to inhabit. For that reason, I strongly encourage you to unplug from television, movies, streaming services, along with everything else the entertainment industry has to offer.

Not only do I strongly encourage you to unplug from those sources, but if you have younger brothers or sisters then you have a sacred duty to see that they also unplug, and to inform your parents of the danger they are in from watching television.

Show this chapter to your parents if you have to. Make a copy of it and hand it to them. You are your brother's keeper and your sister's keeper. If your parents are too busy to research the harmful effects of television, movies, and everything else coming out of the entertainment industry, then it's up to you to inform them. If you don't, and if your younger siblings become corrupted, then the responsibility for their corruption will fall on your shoulders.

You'll be going to hell right along with them.

If you're wondering how things ever got this bad it's because nobody cares. That's the bottom line. Nobody cares. Americans are pudgy and soft people mired in self-pity and fueled by feminine anger and sin.

Life is too short to watch television. Once you unplug and stop watching you're going to have more time in your life for the things that really matter. You're also going to find your intelligence level rising.

It's literally impossible to know anything about the world and how life works while continuing to watch television. Show me someone who watches television, and I'll show a fool who knows nothing about the world. That's really what it boils down to.

Kill your television.

Use a sledgehammer.

Chapter Four

Learn How to Fight

We live in a dangerous world and it's only getting worse. If you're white, the world is especially dangerous. Every time you set foot outside of your house, you're in danger of being attacked or even killed for no reason other than the color of your skin.

Don't expect that to change in your lifetime. The people who run the world hate your guts and they want to see you dead. It's the same if you're a Christian—they hate you and they want to see you dead. In fact, the reason why the people at the top have so much hatred for whites is because they identify white skin with Christian Europe of old.

In order to survive in such a dangerous world, it helps to learn how to fight.

The best way to do that is to pay a visit to your local boxing gym and ask for a couple of lessons. You don't have to spend months working on the speed bag or sparring in the ring. Just tell the instructor you want to learn how to throw some punches and combinations for self-defense in a street fight. He'll know what to show you, so pay attention. And then practice what he teaches you. Hopefully, you'll never have to use it.

If there's no boxing gym in your area, ask the athletic coaches at your school. One of them might be able to show you how to throw a punch.

If your school has a wrestling team, consider joining. Wrestling is great for self-defense; however, it will only work with one attacker at a time. If you're up against multiple attackers, someone could attack you from behind while you're wrestling with somebody else. Of course, there are legendary stories of wrestlers like Dick the Bruiser taking on an entire barroom of opponents. But even he was eventually subdued by eight policemen.

As for sports in general, they can be fun, but they are also a waste of time. How is shooting a basketball or kicking a soccer ball going to help you in the future? With wrestling, you're at least learning a skill that might come in handy someday or even save your life.

Also keep in mind that when you play sports, the school is making money from your participation. They're charging admission for people to attend the games, but you're not seeing a dime of that money, even though you're the star of the show. The school is keeping all of that money for itself.

Another option for self-defense is martial arts. If you go that route, tell the instructor you want to learn some basic self-defense strikes. If you're not upfront with him like that, he'll end up selling you a bunch of classes, along with a pricey uniform and other stuff you don't need. You don't want all that junk. All you want is the ability to survive a street fight.

Aikido is an interesting martial art that focuses on joint locks and throws. Those locks come in handy when you're grappling with an opponent. If you've ever seen a Steven Seagal movie, you've seen combat aikido in action.

Needless to say, I don't recommend ever starting a fight. There's an inherent problem with that advice, as the first punch is 80% of any fight, and sometimes the first punch is the entire fight. So whoever starts the fight usually wins.

Still, I recommend that you be ready to defend yourself, if necessary, but never start a fight or give someone a reason to attack you. For one thing, you never know who you're messing with. If you pick a fight with someone and it turns out they're a trained MMA fighter, you're in trouble. If they have a gun, it's even worse. You could lose your life over some silly little disagreement.

Another reason why I don't recommend starting a fight is morality. You have a right to self-defense, and that right should be invoked if you're ever attacked. But you don't have a right to be the aggressor. Which brings up a third reason why you should never start a fight. . . .

If you're forced to defend yourself and you kill or injure your attacker, you have a legal justification for your actions. Whether or not you still get charged with a crime is an issue we'll discuss a little later. But you do have a legal right to defend yourself.

But if you start a fight and you kill or injure somebody, you could be in for a heap of trouble. Today there are cameras everywhere, not to mention people with cell phones. If you end up in a brawl, the chances are good it's going to be on film somewhere. You won't be able to claim self-defense, if the video shows you started the fight. So your motto is: don't look for trouble, but be ready if trouble finds you.

Fists are Not the Only Way to Fight

In addition to basic boxing and self-defense tactics, it's a good idea to practice a little with weapons, such as pepper spray or mace, and to take a firearms safety class.

Once you know the basics of handling a gun, you're going to have to buy one and the more lethal the better.

For the near future, a handgun should suit your purposes of self-defense. Before you buy one, look into the concealed carry laws where you live. That will influence your choice of what type of gun to purchase.

At some point, depending on whether or not it's legal where you live to do so, you may want to invest in an AK-47, along with plenty of ammo. The AK-47 is the standard infantry weapon in over 100 countries. How powerful of a weapon is it? An army of goat herders in Afghanistan, armed with the AK-47, recently defeated the entire U.S. military. That's how powerful the AK-47 is.

With the United States descending further and further into lawlessness and chaos, being armed is a necessity. That's especially true if you have children.

Should You Be a Hero?

You're walking down the street and see a couple arguing, or worse, a guy slapping a girl around. Should you be a hero and intervene?

What if you're standing in line at the 7-Eleven and some punk comes in with a gun to rob the place? Should you intervene then? It's tricky.

Often in situations like first one if you step in and try to help the girl, both her and the guy slapping her will turn around and attack you.

In the second case, if you step in, even to stop a robbery, you could be arrested and charged with a crime. You can even be arrested and charged in a simple case of self-defense. Somebody could break into your car or into your home and if you exercise your right to self-defense and injure or kill the intruder you could go to jail. If you're white, you're almost certain to be arrested.

Don't think that can't happen, because it has. People have been charged with murder and sent to prison for defending themselves and their families.

In places like London, Sweden, Germany, and South Africa, if an armed criminal—or even a gang of armed criminals—breaks into your home late at night with the intent to murder you and your children, and you kill one of them in self-defense, you will likely be arrested and charged with murder. That's how twisted the world has become.

In those same countries and others, you can get arrested simply for telling the truth. I'm not joking. Telling the truth is literally outlawed in many places throughout the world today. And it's quickly becoming that way in the United States.

You may have heard the term "hate speech." Hate speech is nothing more than telling the truth. It was invented as a means of silencing people and preventing them from telling the truth. It goes hand-in-hand with laws that prevent people from defending themselves from attack.

The end game is control, and outlawing self-defense is part of that control. If leftist politicians had their way, all guns would be outlawed and self-defense in any form would be illegal.

A Dallas County District Attorney recently announced that he will no longer prosecute people who steal personal items worth $750 or less. So if someone breaks into your house and steals your brand new suit, your shoes, or your television, it's not a crime, according to this district attorney, as long as the value is under $750.

His office will determine that the person who stole from you was poor and couldn't afford a new suit, new shoes, or a new television, so all criminal charges against them will be dropped. Even worse, if you arrive home when the theft is taking place and use force to protect your property, *you* will be arrested and charged with a crime.

If someone robs you in a supermarket parking lot and steals all the food you just bought for yourself and your family, this district attorney's office will say that the person who stole from you was hungry and couldn't afford to feed themselves, so no crime was committed. But if you fight with that person and try to prevent them from stealing from you, that same district attorney's office will charge you with assault.

In the city of Seattle, similar action is occurring. Just recently, a man who had been convicted of assault and rape was freed from prison after only nine months, because the judicial system in that city felt his punishment was too harsh.

The man in question immediately returned to the scene of his previous crime and assaulted the same woman he had previously raped. And then he took off. He's on the loose right now, free as a bird.

How would you feel if the woman he raped and assaulted was your sister, your mother, or your wife?

In California, shoplifting is rampant. Mobs of black "youths" descend on a store, grab as much merchandise as they can, and walk out with no fear of arrest. That's because district attorneys all over California have decided it's no longer a crime for people to steal from stores.

If you complain, these same district attorneys will accuse you of hate speech and lock you up for being a racist.

Welcome to America.

How to Fight with Words

You've heard it said that the pen is mightier than the sword. I'm not sure if that's true. Mao Zedong, the late Communist leader of China, said all political power comes from the barrel of a gun. He would know. Communists killed more people in the 20th century, than have died in all of the wars fought throughout history combined—and almost all of those people that the Communists killed were Christians. If you're a Christian, you belong to the most persecuted people in the history of the world.

The Communist overthrow of the United States that we are now living in was also accomplished through the barrel of a gun, via the subversion and takeover of state power: the Justice Department, the FBI, the ATF, the U.S. Military, and police departments all across the country. Still, words are powerful. It's to your benefit to learn how to speak and write with power.

If your school offers debate classes or classes in public speaking, take them, and become good at it. If your school has a debate team, join it, and become the best debater on the team.

Learning to speak and debate publicly is a valuable skill. The only downside to taking such classes at your school is that you will be assigned to take the wrong side of various topics. You will be asked to argue in favor of gun control, or to take the pro-murder side and argue in favor of abortion.

Mentally ill teachers love doing this—they love forcing students to argue in favor of their own sick and twisted agendas. If you're put in that position, you have two choices. You can politely refuse to debate that particular side of an argument, or you can go ahead with the assignment, using the talking points of whatever the issue is as a way of learning how the enemy thinks and speaks. If you choose to go forward with the assignment, be careful not to get sucked into falling for the wrong side.

In addition to learning how to speak and debate in public, take some writing classes. Take a typing class, if you don't already know how, and take classes in composition, grammar, essay writing, and creative writing. The classes might be boring, but if you force yourself to learn how to write, it will benefit you tremendously as an adult. If you become skilled at fighting with words, you will be an extremely rare individual; a person of power in the upper echelon of humanity.

An Ounce of Prevention is Worth a Pound of Cure

It's a crazy world we live in. To avoid trouble, you need to be constantly aware of everything going on around you.

Mind your own business. Most people will leave you alone if you treat them with respect, which often means keeping your mouth shut.

Don't let anyone you don't know get behind you. If someone does, calmly turn to the side and keep them in your peripheral vision. If their intent was to harm you, they'll know that they've now lost the element of surprise.

I can't tell you how many times the simple act of being aware has prevented someone from trying to rob or attack me. In one instance, it saved my life when some punk tried pulling the Knockout Game on me.

The Knockout Game isn't a game at all. It's a black guy sneaking up on a white person and sucker punching them from behind when they're not looking. It's called the Knockout Game, because the goal is for the thug to knock out his victim with one punch. The people who do this usually pick on a woman or an old person who can't defend themselves, but it could be anyone who's not paying attention and doesn't see the attacker sneaking up on them.

In my case, I was standing alone on a subway platform at five o'clock in the morning when out of the corner of my eye, I saw a black guy running at me with his fist up. I turned as quickly as I could and threw my arm up to block his punch. That move on my part saved my life, because if he'd have hit me, I'd have fallen to the tracks and been hit by a train.

I swung back at him, but having lost the element of surprise, he immediately ran away. You can read a fictionalized retelling of that attack in my book *Based: A Young Adult Novel about Race, Dating, and Growing Up in America.*

Another time, a punk followed me and hid behind the side of a vending machine that I stopped to use. He was waiting for me to pull some money out of my pocket so he could rob me. He thought I didn't see him, but I knew he was there.

Because I knew he was there, I braced myself. As soon as he made his move, I was going to slam his head through the front of that vending machine so hard it would have cracked the entire front of the machine.

He peeped out to look at me and realized I was aware of his presence. Then he chickened out. That was an attempted robbery thwarted, thanks to situational awareness.

Those are just two of the many examples I could list for you. In most cases, being aware will prevent an attack from occurring. In the rare case where an attack does occur, being aware will leave you ready to respond.

Some things are worth fighting for, such as defending yourself or your family. Other things aren't, like an insult from some punk you don't know and will probably never see again. Learn to understand the difference.

Don't play with your phone in public like girls do.

Be aware of your surroundings at all times.

Lock your doors, both at home and in your car.

Don't leave anything visible lying on your car seat.

Don't flaunt your money or brag about it.

Be careful when taking money out of your pocket and don't let anyone see it. It might give them ideas.

Be careful when using an ATM. If you see suspicious characters around, wait until later or go to another ATM.

Don't open your door to strangers.

Don't engage in conversation with strangers.

Limit or even avoid interaction with men of different races than yours. Be polite, but don't engage in unnecessary conversation and don't spend time with them.

Don't relax around men of a different race unless you know them. If you see two or more men of a different race, be careful. If they look even the slightest bit suspicious, be extra careful.

Don't look men of other races in the eye when you pass by them. Otherwise, you'll be met with, "What the **** you looking at?" followed by an attack. But do keep them in your peripheral vision in case they attack anyway and be extra careful.

Don't arrange to meet with anyone of a different race in order to buy or sell something.

Don't partner in business or involve yourself in deals with anyone of a different race.

Don't act the Good Samaritan and intervene in disputes or fights between people of a different race. Never, ever, ever, no matter what you see.

Don't attend parties, bars, movies, nightclubs, or any sort of social gathering where male members of a different race might gather. Just. Don't. Do it.

There's no shortage of mentally ill women and feminized men who will dispute the above advice and falsely claim that people of all races are the same. Anyone who believes that ranks among the dumbest of the dumb.

The truth is that humans are alike in the sense that they all laugh, cry, and feel pain; however, there are startling differences among the races in terms of character, personality, and intelligence.

If anyone tells you otherwise, you can prove they are wrong with a simple challenge. Tell them to take a walk around their neighborhood at night, while nodding and saying hi to everyone they pass.

Then tell them to repeat the exercise the following night, only instead of taking a stroll around their own neighborhood, tell them to drive to the nearest Democrat-controlled city and take a walk down Avenue K, nodding and smiling at every person they pass.

You'll be met with a stuttering, spittle-flying display of spastic rage. But not one of them will have the courage to take you up on your challenge. Not one. They know if they did, they'd be raped, robbed, or murdered.

Rather than admit the obvious truth, they'll take their anger and fear out on you. That's your proof that the person you're talking to is nothing more than a moronic, demon-possessed liar.

Don't ignore the advice in this chapter. It's some of the best advice anyone will ever give you, and that no one else has ever given you before. It's advice that could very likely save your life.

According to the Bureau of Justice Statistics, there were 562,000 violent interracial incidents in 2019 alone, and 84% of them consisted of violence against white people. 84% of

562,000 is 473,000. That's 1,295 violent attacks against white people every day; violent attacks committed by members of other races for no reason other than an intense hatred of white people.

As we said at the beginning of this chapter, if you're white, there are millions of people who want to see you dead. You've never hurt or harmed them in any way, but they hate you nonetheless and want to kill you. That's just the way it is in 21st century America. Don't listen to anyone who tells you different.

If you're unable to learn any type of self-tactics or if your parents won't let you, you're going to have to go out of your way to avoid trouble. You should be doing that anyway, but you'll have to be extra careful. Be as polite as you can, avoid any situation or place where trouble might be brewing, and keep your eyes open.

Bodybuilding as Self-Defense

One excellent way to prevent trouble from starting is by building your body. If you're strong and look strong, people tend to leave you alone. I don't know of anyone other than myself who has ever made this connection between bodybuilding and self-defense. But to me that connection is obvious. Bodybuilding is a deterrent to assault.

To better understand this, consider that predators, both human and animal, share a common trait: They pick on the weak. After all, why should a predator risk injury or even death by attacking an opponent who is capable of fighting back, when they could just as easily find an opponent that is weak and unlikely to offer any meaningful resistance? That's how predators act.

If you're currently being bullied or picked on at school, then bodybuilding is one of the best things you could possibly do. As your muscles start to grow, those same bullies will start leaving you alone. They'll look for someone smaller and weaker to pick on.

There are some low-level animal types with no impulse control who will attack both the strong and the weak. But those cases are rare. Most predators will leave a strong person alone.

Bodybuilding then is something you should actively participate in. You don't need weights and you don't need to join any type of gym. You can build your body better and faster without them. To learn the best way to do that, read the next chapter.

NOTE: If you took the fake vaccine for the phone virus, don't engage in boxing, wrestling, or any other physical exercise. I'll have more to say about this in the next chapter. For now just be aware that it is simply too dangerous for you to tax your heart or your stress level in any way. I'm sorry to be the one to tell you that, but I promised to give it to you straight in this book. So I am.

Chapter Five

Build Your Body Fast and Easy

Are you ready for some muscle? Before we get into some specific exercises that are going to build your body fast, there are two other factors we need to discuss: nutrition and sleep. They are just as important as exercise when it comes to building muscle.

Think of your bodybuilding program as a tripod or three-legged stool. The three legs of that tripod are nutrition, sleep, and exercise. If all three legs are strong, your results will be fast and immediate. But if you remove only one of those three legs, the entire enterprise will topple over.

We're going to start with the first leg, nutrition. I know some of you are eager to jump right to the exercises, but remember—all three legs of your program are important. If I start with the exercises, some of you won't bother to read the information on nutrition and sleep, and that will slow your progress.

Vince Gironda was an old-time bodybuilder, trainer, and gym owner known as the Iron Guru. One of Vince's rules was that bodybuilding is 80% nutrition. Most experts tend to agree with him. Your muscles need nourishment to grow. Specifically, they need protein from animal sources. Vince insisted that meat, fish, milk, and eggs were the real muscle builders.

I don't recommend consuming milk or dairy products that are pasteurized, because while they might be beneficial for building muscle, the pasteurization process destroys almost all of the key nutrients those foods contain. In fact, from a health standpoint, pasteurized dairy products are one of the worst things you can put into your body.

Raw milk and dairy products are a different story. If you have access to raw dairy products, then I wholeheartedly recommend them. Unfortunately, I think Texas and California are the only states in the country right now where raw milk and raw dairy products are legal to buy.

If you don't have access to raw milk and raw dairy products, your best protein sources will be wild, ocean-caught fish, such as wild salmon (not farm raised) or wild mackerel; beef and liver from grass-fed animals (not grain fed); fertile eggs from pastured chickens (not caged chickens), and liver.

Don't neglect eating liver, because you don't like the taste. Beef liver from grass-fed animals is nature's multi-vitamin; the most nutritious food on the planet. Raw liver (frozen for at least two weeks) from clean sources can restore energy and vitality to even the most exhausted organism.

How much protein do you need? If you consume from 80 to 120 grams of protein a day, you will gain muscle rapidly. An average egg contains 6 grams of protein. Four ounces of meat or fish contain roughly 20 grams of protein. A glass of raw milk contains 8 grams of protein. If you consume three meals a day of 25-30 grams of protein each, or four meals a day of 20-25 grams of protein each, you'll be okay.

In addition to protein, you want to consume organic fruits and vegetables. Fruits are best eaten alone in snacks. Don't eat fruit with protein or with vegetables. Protein, starches, and fruits require different enzymes in order to digest properly. Starches and fruits should always be eaten separately and not at the same time as other foods.

Vegetables, particularly green vegetables, such as broccoli, lettuce, asparagus, etc., can be eaten with your protein. Vegetables can also be juiced. It takes a while to get used to the taste of raw celery juice, raw cucumber juice, or raw carrot juice, but those juices are loaded with nutrients.

Ideally, you want to consume three to four meals a day, each one consisting of one protein source and possibly one or two vegetables. You can include a fruit snack between meals if you get hungry. Ripe bananas (yellow with a few small brown spots on them) are great for snacks. Just be sure to eat them alone, at least four hours after a meal, or one hour before a meal.

If you have access to raw milk, drink it alone about an hour before meals. Don't drink it with your meals. In fact, don't drink any liquid with your meals. Instead, consume liquids an hour before eating. This is especially important if you are overweight.

Chew your food slowly when you eat and take your time. Make your meals as pleasurable as possible. With each mouthful of food you consume, think about how that food is going to fuel your muscles and make them grow.

Foods to avoid are anything that contains sugar, as well as anything that comes in a bottle, box, jar, bag, wrapper, or can. Basically anything that's processed or is not organically grown. Don't eat soy or synthetic meat alternatives. Avoid all fast food.

When you buy produce, look at the little numbered sticker. If you see a 5-digit number, beginning with the number 9, then the produce is organic. That's what you want.

If you see a 4-digit number, beginning with the number 4, then the produce is conventional, which means it was grown with pesticides. That's what you don't want. But if you're stuck, you're stuck. Conventional produce with peels, like bananas and oranges, are not as bad as produce without peels, like apples. I eat conventional Dole bananas on occasion, as well as conventional broccoli that's well rinsed. But they're never my first choice.

If you see a 5-digit number beginning with the number 8, then the produce is Genetically Modified. That's what you absolutely do not want, under any circumstances.

Don't drink or cook with tap water. It is unfit for human consumption. The best water is distilled. If you add the juice of a lemon to a gallon of distilled water, it becomes great to drink. Avoid soda, beer, coffee, and all soft drinks.

I realize that eating for muscles is a tall order, so do the best you can. Don't stress out if you have to consume conventional (non-organic) produce from time to time, or if you decide to eat in a restaurant, or if you're stuck eating the slop they feed you in school; just do the best you can.

You might have to search or have your parents do a little searching in order to locate wild, ocean-caught fish; beef and liver from grass fed animals; and organic produce. But it's well worth the effort. You'll feel and look better, think clearer, and your muscles with have plenty of fuel to grow on.

Say No to Drugs

Needless to say, you want to avoid all alcohol, cigarettes, and drugs. When I say drugs, I mean all drugs, particularly vaccines. Never let anyone give you a shot or a vaccination for anything under any circumstances.

If your parents forced you to take the jab for the phony pandemic, you're not in a good spot. There's a possibility that you got the placebo (a saline solution and not the real thing), so you can hope that's the case. Whatever you do, don't ever take another shot ever again. If someone comes at you with a needle, tell them to back off. If they refuse, you have the right to use as much force as necessary to repel them, including deadly force.

By the way, did you know that the Bible teaches that all drugs are sorcery and witchcraft? It's true. There's a book called *Strong's Concordance*, which contains the Hebrew and Greek translations for every word in both the Old and New Testament in the Bible. If you take that book, and put it next to your Bible, and then open your Bible to Revelations 18:23, and look at the last sentence, it reads, "For thy merchants were the great men of the earth, for by thy sorceries were all nations deceived."

Then open your *Strong's Concordance* to the Main Concordance and find the word "sorceries." Scroll down the list under that word to Revelations 18:23 or Re 18:23. Next to that it will say, "by thy *s* were all nations deceived," followed by the number 5331. Turn to the back of the book where the Greek translations are, locate that same number, and you'll see that it says, "pharmakeia from 5332; medication ("pharmacy"), i.e. magic, sorcery, witchcraft."

If you scroll down a couple of lines, you'll see that it also says, "Pharmakon; a druggist or poisoner, i.e. a magician, sorcerer."

The Bible has always taught that drugs are sorcery and that those who dispense them are sorcerers, witches and poisoners. Weak-willed women and feminized men don't want to admit that because they're cowards and prefer to hide from the truth, but there it is. Now you know the truth.

Stay away from alcohol, especially beer. Beer is literally liquid estrogen. Estrogen is a female sex hormone. Every time you drink beer, you're flooding your body with female sex hormones. It's disgusting and one of the worst things a man can do.

If you are underweight and looking to increase the size of your muscles, you're going to have to eat more. That doesn't mean stuffing yourself; it means to gradually increase both the frequency of your meals, as well as the amount of food you consume.

If you're currently eating twice a day, increase that to three or four times a day. If you're eating three times a day, increase that to four or five times a day. Slowly increase the amount of food you eat. If you eat two eggs every day for breakfast, increase that to three eggs every day for one or two weeks. Then increase it to four eggs every day, and then to five eggs, etc.

If you are overweight, do the opposite. Cut down on the amount of food you eat, as well as the frequency. However, don't eat less than three times a day. Your muscles need fuel to grow.

Proper nutrition is vital to your bodybuilding progress, so don't neglect it. Trying to grow muscles on a diet of sugar, soda, candy, pastries, cereal, white bread, ice cream, fast food hamburgers, French fries, and all-around junk is a daunting task. I'm not saying it's impossible, but it is extremely difficult. Why put yourself behind the eight ball when you're just starting out?

If you really want to study up on nutrition, there's a marvelous book called *Nutrition and Physical Degeneration* by Dr. Weston Price that might be available at your local library.

Dr. Price was a dentist who traveled around the world in the 1930s, studying the teeth and general health of indigenous people (people native to a land). What he found was startling: indigenous people, eating a natural diet with no processed food whatsoever, had excellent dental health and strong, physically fit bodies.

They had no cancer and no heart disease. Many of their communities had no police department or jail, because there was no need for them. However, when they began eating processed food, imported by explorers and settlers, everything changed.

Their health deteriorated rapidly. Crime and delinquency became problems. Cancer, heart disease, and other illnesses that had been nonexistent before, suddenly appeared. The same food that most Americans consume on a daily basis destroyed these people. Don't let it do the same to you.

If you want perfect teeth and the strongest, most muscular body possible, then one of the best pieces of advice I can give you is to read Dr. Price's book and follow his diet recommendations. There's only one problem. The book is extremely long and it makes for some pretty stiff reading.

A far more efficient way to absorb Dr. Price's research is to read the book *Cure Tooth Decay* by Ramiel Nagel, available on the internet. It's an excellent summary of Dr. Price's work and it's very easy to read.

If your parents are giving you a hard time about the kind of food you want to eat, give them a copy of *Cure Tooth Decay,* so they can study the research themselves. As I write this, the book is currently selling for around $20.

Nutrition is the first leg on your tripod of success. Sleep is the second leg.

Sleep Your Way to Success

Your muscles need rest in order to grow, so do your best to sleep from eight to ten hours a night. If that's not possible, then try to get at least seven hours of sleep. Less than seven hours a night is pushing it. It's possible to get by on less than seven hours of sleep a night. I've done it for long periods, but I don't recommend it, especially for a teen.

Be aware that healing and muscle growth occur when you sleep. Your muscles don't grow when you are awake and they don't grow when you are exercising; they grow when you are sleeping.

Healing and muscle growth actually take place during the REM (Rapid Eye Movement) phase of sleeping. REM sleep is when you are dreaming and the more time you spend sleeping the more of the REM phase you experience. If you're sick or if you want to grow muscle, or even grow taller, the best thing you can do is sleep.

HGH (Human Growth Hormone) is released primarily when you sleep. HGH promotes tissue repair and skin rejuvenation.

For guys, sleep is a natural alternative to steroids. In fact, old-time bodybuilding coaches used to recommend sleeping after a workout. They called it a "muscle nap" and they advised their trainees to workout, consume nutritious protein, and then take a nap. That's not always practical in the real world, but if you can do it, why not? The truth is the more you sleep, the faster your muscles will grow and the quicker your entire body will heal from any illness you have.

Personally, I function best with ten hours of sleep a night. You might need a little more or a little less.

When you sleep is almost as important as how much. There are certain growth processes that occur in the body from 10 PM to 2 AM that don't occur at any other time, and they only take place when you are sleeping, not when you are awake. So you have to be asleep during those hours in order to benefit.

There are other processes that occur from 2 AM to 6 AM. You have to be asleep during those hours for those growth processes to occur. They won't happen if you're awake.

In order to give your body all of the ammunition it needs to heal and grow it's important for you to be in bed and sleeping every night from 10 PM to 6 AM. Even better would be to sleep from 9 PM to 7 AM.

Did you know that sleep deprivation is a form of torture? It's true. If you want to drive a person crazy, the easiest way to do that is to deprive that person of sleep.

Today, almost the entire population of the world is chronically sleep-deprived. Not to the extreme that would be labeled torture, but certainly enough to create disease in the body, and certainly enough to prevent the body from operating at peak efficiency.

Sleep helps with depression. There's no better way to escape your troubles than sleep. Life got you down? Try taking a nap. You'll feel much better when you wake up.

It might not be possible for you to always get the proper amount of sleep. If that's the case, do the best you can.

You'll find it easier to enjoy restful sleep if you make your bedroom as quiet and as comfortable as possible. 100% cotton sheets and bed clothes will help.

If you have trouble falling asleep, here's a great tip: try eliminating all sound for thirty minutes before you go to bed. By that, I mean no talking, no music, no television, no sound at all. Your mind will quiet down and you'll find it easy to nod off and enjoy a restful night's sleep.

Also, make sure your bed is comfortable and your room is quiet. If your neighbors are noisy and refuse to quiet down, you have two choices: you can move or you can buy a $20 box fan made by Lasko.

Place the fan near your bed and aim it at the wall so it's not blowing all over you. Your purpose in buying the fan is to create ambient noise. The quiet whir of the fan will do that.

Hopefully, it will be loud enough to drown out your neighbors.

If you have trouble keeping light out of your bedroom, invest in an inexpensive sleep mask. Your body will thank you. Remember, your body grows, repairs, and regenerates while you are sleeping.

No one ever gets it right all the time, so take comfort knowing that a little improvement is better than no improvement.

In addition to sleep, practice resting throughout the day. If you're trying to pack muscle on your body, then you can't be running around and involved in all different kinds of activities. You can participate in sports, such as baseball, basketball, football, wrestling, etc., but don't overdo it.

Also, I would not recommend long distance running. Running one mile, two miles, maybe even five miles is okay. But people who run marathons are extremely weak and thin.

Now for a big one: emotional stress.

It's really hard to gain muscle when you're under emotional stress. It can be done, but it's not easy. The kind of emotional stress I'm talking about is dealing with parents, school and government bureaucracy, friends (so-called), and girls.

We'll discuss girls a little later in this book. As far as school goes, you have enough information now to know just how badly your teachers are lying to you. You don't have to confront them over every lie. You can, but you don't have to. I can tell you right now they aren't going to listen to a word you say, no matter how convincing. You could shower them with facts, evidence, and logic, and it won't mean a hill of beans. Their minds are made up and no amount of truthful information is going to change it. I recommend homeschooling, which we'll also talk about a little later.

In the meantime, practice calming your mind. Maintain poise at all times. Never let your emotions get the better of you, and don't allow your emotions to dictate your actions.

Watch your anger. Anger, particularly emotional anger, is a feminine characteristic. When you see someone engage in emotionalized anger, you're seeing someone in possession of a weak, feminine spirit. Don't be like them.

Getting your diet and sleep requirements right will take care of the first two legs of your tripod of health, strength, and muscle. The third leg—the one you've been waiting for—is exercise.

Weights or No Weights?

Are weights and machines necessary in order to build your body?

No, they are not.

Weights and machines can be useful tools for building your body, but they are absolutely not necessary. And as someone who has trained both with and without weights, it's my contention that you can make better, faster, and more fulfilling progress in building your body without weights.

I'm not the only person whose experience reflects that. A friend of mine has a twin brother, and as teenagers they both got hooked on the muscle bug. What makes their case interesting is that they each followed a different path to their goal.

One brother went on a standard bodybuilding program using weights. His exercises consisted of barbell curls, squats, military presses and bench presses, along with some dumbbell work. His twin brother trained without weights and followed a routine like the one you're going to read about in this book.

After three months, which brother do you think made the most noticeable progress? It was the twin who followed an exercise program like the one in this book, a program without weights. In fact, the difference in results that each brother achieved was striking.

The brother who followed the standard bodybuilding program with weights looked better than he had three months ago. He was more muscular and certainly in better shape.

But his twin brother, the one who trained without weights, literally transformed himself. He looked like a Hercules in the making after only three months.

Now let me tell you what happened in my case.

When I was 15-years-old, the strongest kid in my grade was a guy named Marshall W.

Marshall was built like a moose, with a powerful chest and legs like tree trunks. He was also the only person in my sophomore class that played on the varsity football team with guys that were 17 and 18-years-old.

All of the varsity football players were on a supervised strength-training program with weights, using an old Universal weight machine, and their maximum lifts were posted on a wall in the boys' locker room, just above the door to the coach's office.

There, in the musty-smelling locker room, you could look up and see everyone's one-rep maximum in the bench press and squat. Some of the older guys could bench 260 to 270 pounds. Marshall's best bench press was 225 pounds, which is a lot of weight and very impressive for a 15-year-old to bench press.

Most adult men can't bench press 200 pounds, let alone 225 pounds. In fact, over 90% of the adult men in the world today, including many who weigh over 200 pounds would get crushed if they tried to bench 225 pounds. Marshall could do it and he weighed 180 pounds.

As for me, I wasn't on the football team, and I didn't have access to any kind of supervised strength-training program or any program involving weights at all.

What I had was the program contained in this book.

I trained on that program for 15-20 minutes, three days a week for three full months and literally transformed my body, going from 140 pounds at a height of 5'9", to 170 pounds. That's when I decided to test myself on the weights.

One day, after my morning P.E. class, instead of rushing to change clothes like everyone else, I hurried into the weight room to see how much I could bench press.

I started with 100 pounds. The weight shot up and lowered with a clang. I was shocked at how easy it was. It literally felt like nothing. As I had never done a bench press before, balancing the weight was harder than the weight itself. Quickly, I added weight and tried again. Same result. More weight. Same result. I was going to be late for my next class, but I wasn't leaving that weight room until I knew exactly how strong I'd become.

I kept adding weight, resting only seconds between each new attempt. When I went over 180 pounds, the weight felt heavy, but I still managed it.

The bell rang, signaling that I was now officially late for my next class, but I didn't care.

I went over 200 pounds, gripped the handles tight, and pushed it up. I was breathing like a steam engine, but I had to make one last attempt.

I loaded 225 pounds, slid into place, and pressed the weight all the way up.

Despite not training with weights at all, I was now officially as strong as Marshall, the strongest kid in my class, and one of the strongest kids in the entire class.

I had no one to share my success with, but inside I was bursting with pride. I had accomplished something wonderful, and I had done it entirely on my own, using the exercise routine you're going to read about in this book.

Fast, Fun and Effective

The exercise routine I'm about to recommend is based on the three "F"s: Fast, Fun, and Effective. It's also safe, which is a fourth "F".

It's fast in two ways. First, in the sense that it will only take you around 15-20 minutes to perform. And second, in how quickly you are going to see results.

Follow this routine faithfully, and you're going to see muscle growth not in months, not in weeks, but literally within days. Stick with it for three months and you're going to create an entirely new body.

These exercises are fun in that they are easy to do, and once you see the results they deliver, you'll never want to stop doing them. There's no pain involved, only the thrill of physical exertion.

You can do these exercises alone in your room, in your basement, wherever.

Nobody has to see you. They're totally safe.

This routine is effective. It's guaranteed to give you the utmost in bodybuilding results in the shortest possible time, and it has never been known to fail.

Not once. Not ever.

It's turned scrawny human scarecrows into mountains of muscle. It's turned boys into men. It's done all that and more. So buckle up and enjoy the ride.

Getting Started

Let me give you a few quick tips before we begin.

First, train three days a week, with a day of rest in between workouts.

Your workouts will generally take around 20 minutes to perform. If you want to stretch your muscles before you start or train at a more leisurely pace, that's fine. In that case, your workout will take you around 30 minutes to perform. Just don't overdo it. Don't think that by training longer you'll make better progress. Your muscles grow when they are resting, not when they are being used.

That's a hard concept for many people to grasp, but it makes perfect sense when you think about it. First you stimulate your muscles with exercise, and then they grow while you are resting. Remember, muscle growth occurs while you sleep.

Some people like to listen to music when they train, others like silence. You can try both ways and see what works best for you.

Wear loose clothing when you train. If you're exercising at home, it's best to do it barefoot.

Don't hold your breath when exercising. Continue to breathe, exhaling at the point of exertion—when you are pushing or pulling against resistance, and inhaling when you are lowering the resistance.

When you perform an exercise, it's called a repetition, and a group of repetitions is called a set. Thus, if you perform an exercise five times, it would be called five repetitions—or five reps, for short—for one set. It would be written as 1 x 5.

If you did five reps, rested a minute or two, and then did another five reps, it would be called two sets of five reps, and it would be written as 2 x 5.

One thing you'll notice is your muscles pumping up. That happens when blood fills the muscle and causes it to swell. It's actually a pleasurable feeling, one that you'll get hooked on.

Bodybuilding is a solitary journey. Don't compare yourself or your results to others. You're not in competition with them; you're in competition with yourself. So strive to better yourself and leave others alone to do the same.

As I mentioned earlier, when I first performed this program, I was 15-years-old, and weighed 140 pounds at a height of 5'9". Three months later, I weighed 170 pounds with shoulders so wide everyone I knew was shocked.

Your results might be similar or they might be greater than mine. Part of the fun is seeing just how far you can go.

The Upper Body Squat

Your upper body routine will consist of two primary exercises: Jackknife Pushups and Chin-Ups, along with some flexing and tension exercises.

If you don't have access to a chin-up bar, don't worry. You can either skip the exercise or find a way to improvise.

Most schools have a chin-up bar somewhere on the premises. If you can sneak off and do a set or two while no one is around, great. You can also rig up a bar at home. In my case, I found an eight foot metal bar that someone was throwing away next to a dumpster.

I took it home and found a place in my kitchen where I could lay one end of the bar across a shelf in one of the cabinets, and then lay the other end across a shelf in another cabinet about six feet away. It was slightly uneven, so I put some magazines under the low end until the bar was level. Since then, I've had a chin-up bar.

Once you start bodybuilding, you'll find that you can improvise just about any exercise.

The first exercise in your routine is the Jackknife Pushup. This exercise is so effective and so result-producing that I call it the upper body squat.

Bodybuilders who train with weights consider squats performed with a barbell across the upper back to be the most result-producing of all exercises. In fact, barbell squats have such a successful history when it comes to building muscle they've achieved almost legendary status. Those who promote barbell squats are right in one sense. Barbell squats are an effective exercise when it comes to building muscle, however, they also produce tremendous compression on the spine, and for that reason I do *not* recommend them.

In fact, I would make the argument that spinal compression produced by barbell squats will prevent a person from growing to their full height. In other words, they will stunt your growth. And that's the last thing you want.

Jackknife Pushups will do for your upper body— specifically for your shoulders—what barbell squats do for the lower body and back, only in total safety and without compressing your spine.

I consider Jackknife Pushups to be the King of upper body exercises. They're certainly the king of upper body exercises when it comes to thickening and broadening your shoulders. Your shoulders are going to grow so wide from doing this exercise, that you will literally be shocked.

To perform a Jackknife Pushup, assume a position similar to a pushup, only with your butt high in the air. In other words, your feet will be close together and touching; your hands will be flat on the floor, a little wider than shoulder width apart; and your hips will be pointed up towards the ceiling, in an upside down V. With your eyes focused on your feet, you will feel like you're upside down.

From this position, bend your arms and slowly lower your head to the floor. Touch your head lightly to the floor (don't bang your head) and then press back up. You should feel this exercise in your shoulders. The average person will be able to do around eight repetitions of this exercise. For your first workout, do five or six repetitions. Immediately after finishing your set, lower yourself to your knees, and while kneeling on the floor, extend your hands to your sides, elbows bent and palms up.

Pretend you have a heavy log resting on the palms of your hands and strive to push it up, only don't move your hands. Imagine you are pushing against the log and feel the tension in your shoulders. Do this for several seconds. This is a great tension exercise for the shoulders.

Every time you finish a set of Jackknife Pushups, do several seconds of this tension exercise. Between the Jackknife Pushups and the tension exercises, your shoulders are going to pump full of blood.

Once you get the hang of doing Jackknife Pushups, you can experiment with your hand position, moving your hands a little closer together or a little further apart. Do what feels best for you and what produces the best feeling (the best pump) in your shoulders.

You can also experiment with the way you lower your head to the floor. You can try touching your forehead to the floor or touching the top of your head. Touching your forehead is a little easier, but touching the top of your head puts more tension on the shoulders. Again, use what works best for you.

Do the same with the tension exercise by experimenting with different hand widths.

For your first workout, do a set of five or six reps of Jackknife Pushups, rest a minute or two, and then do a second set. And follow each set with the tension exercise for your shoulders.

If five reps are too many for you, then just do one or two.

If you can't do any reps at all, just hold the top position for as long as you can and/or try lowering yourself a couple of inches at a time until you are able to complete a full rep.

Remember, you're competing with yourself, not with anyone else. So don't feel bad if you struggle at first. Your progress will come very fast.

For your first week, do two sets of Jackknife Pushups, followed by the tension exercise. Rest a minute or two between sets.

For your second and third week, do three sets with a minute or two of rest between each one. For your fourth week, do four sets. Four sets will be your max.

Try to add a rep or even a couple of reps each workout until you are doing four sets of twenty repetitions. By then, if you've eaten enough nutritious food and gotten enough sleep, your shoulders will be anywhere from one to three inches wider than they are now. That's a lot of muscle.

Once you are doing four sets of twenty repetitions, stay at that level for a couple of weeks and then begin making the exercise progressively harder by doing your last set with your feet on a small stool or chair, around 12-15 inches high.

That angle will make the exercise much more difficult as you will now be lowering and pressing up more bodyweight than before. You will probably have to start that last set at five reps and then build up again. You may also need to start resting three or four minutes between sets.

When you are able to do fifteen to twenty repetitions on your last set with your feet raised, start doing your third set the same way.

When you are able to do fifteen to twenty repetitions on your last two sets with your feet raised, start doing your second set the same way.

Eventually, you will reach the point where you are doing one set the normal way, with your feet on the floor, for twenty repetitions; followed by three sets of fifteen to twenty repetitions with your feet raised. And you will be doing several seconds of the tension exercise after each set of Jackknife Pushups. At this point, your shoulders are going to be extremely wide.

Stay at this level for a few weeks, and then increase the progression by doing your last set with your feet on a slightly higher surface, and then work your way up as before.

Every now and then, you can go back to doing all four sets with your feet on the floor for a light workout. It's good for the body to mix things up. An occasional light workout is not a bad idea.

It's also a good idea to take a full week off with no exercise every four months. The rest will do your body good.

So that's your core upper body exercise: the Jackknife Pushup. The second exercise in your program is Chin-Ups.

Chin-Ups are pretty self-explanatory. You grip the bar and pull yourself up until your chin clears the bar. Then you lower yourself down, stopping before you reach a full extension at the bottom, and then pull up again.

Grip the bar with your *palms facing you*, hands about shoulder width apart. Feel your biceps contract at the top of the movement when your chin clears the bar. Chin-Ups done in this manner will build your biceps like no other exercise. They are much better than barbell curls.

Think of it this way: if you weigh 160 pounds and are able to do a chin-up, you've just moved 160 pounds, primarily with the strength of your biceps. Yet how many people are able to do curls with 160 pounds? Almost nobody.

Perform two sets. Similar to Jackknife Pushups, you can experiment with different hand widths. I do my first set with my hands around shoulder width apart, and my second set with my hands from six to ten inches apart.

When you do Chin-Ups, look up at the ceiling, not straight ahead, and think of pulling your elbows down and back.

It's okay to swing your legs out in front of you as you pull up. Doing so will allow you to pull yourself higher.

After each set of Chin-Ups, you're going to do a flexing exercise for your biceps. Hold your right arm out to the side of your head, as if you were going to make a muscle. You've seen plenty of athletes and musclemen do this when they flex their biceps. Do the same thing only don't clench your fist. Instead, keep your hand open and twist your thumb back and up.

You should feel a contraction in your bicep. Hold this for a few seconds and then clench your fist and flex your bicep conventionally. Do the same for your left arm.

If you have trouble feeling this exercise, try touching your ear with your little finger and then turning your thumb back and up. Again, you should feel a contraction in your bicep. You can also try doing this with your hand behind your head.

You want to feel the bicep muscle contract, bulge, and flex, and then try to expand or bulge it out even more.

Chin-Ups with your palms facing you, followed by the flexing exercise will build your biceps very rapidly. Start with two sets of one or two reps in Chin-Ups and build up from there. You'll see some solid growth when you are able to do four reps, and when you can do two sets of six reps, you are really getting somewhere. At that point, you can do three sets if you want. Only don't do it if it feels like too much.

If you can't perform a single rep, try hanging from the bar for increasing lengths of time, along with pulling yourself up an inch or two. Gradually increase the height you are able to pull until you can do a full rep. It might take a few weeks. It might take few months. But eventually, you'll get there.

To build your forearms, add an additional set or two, only do them with your *palms facing away from you* and your hands three or four inches apart. Chin-Ups done that way will build your forearms. You can build forearms as big and sinewy as Popeye's with a couple of sets done that way.

If you don't have access to a chin-up bar at home, but you do have one at your school or place of employment, then it's okay to do your Chin-Ups on their own for a couple of sets, and then do your Jackknife Pushups at a different time when you are home. You don't have to do the two exercises at the same time, or even on the same day.

If you don't have access to a chin-up bar at all, and you are unable to improvise an alternative, just do the flexing exercise for your biceps. You can build great size in your biceps with that exercise alone.

Now if you promise to get enough sleep and eat enough food, I'll give you an exercise for your triceps, which is the muscle on the back of your upper arm.

It's a simple movement, a pushup done on the floor, only with your hands closer together than in a normal pushup, about twelve inches apart, and close to your lower chest. Your legs and feet should be together. As you lower your body, your elbows should flare back, putting the tension on your triceps. Try it until you get the hang of it. You won't be able to do many reps, so start with what you can do and build up.

Do one or two sets of this triceps exercise after your Chin-ups and then do a tension exercise for your triceps. Hold your arm at your side, and then consciously straighten your triceps by pulling the muscle up. At the same time, raise your shoulder towards your ear. You should feel the muscle on the back of your arm tighten and contract. Hold that feeling for about six seconds, and then do the same with your other arm.

For the rest of your body, we are going to do flexing and tension exercises. You can do these tension exercises every day as they are extremely easy to recover from.

Don't hold your breath when doing these exercises, or when doing any exercise.

Always continue to breathe.

For your chest (pectoral muscle), stand naturally, and then bring your shoulders and arms down and in. Your pectoral muscles will bulge and flex. You can do one side at a time if you want or you can do both pecs at the same time. Hold for six seconds.

You can also bend forward at your waist and push down towards the floor with your hands, while contracting your pectoral muscles. Or stand upright and expand your chest outward, trying to bulge your pectoral muscles out as far as possible.

For your stomach, bend forward slightly and blow all the air out of your lungs. Then pull your belly button in until it touches your backbone. Obviously, you won't be able to do that, but that's the feeling you want. Hold for about six seconds.

This exercise is called a Stomach Vacuum. It won't build your abdominal (stomach) muscles, but it will shrink your waist. Perform this exercise every day after you wake up, and also just before every meal. No one needs to know you are doing it.

To build abdominal muscle, take a breath and then exhale slowly while flexing and tensing your stomach muscles.

For your calf muscle, place one leg slightly in front of the other and then with the leg in front lift your heel and feel your calf muscle contract tightly. Hold for six seconds and try to push that calf muscle out as far as it will go. Do the same with your other leg. Be careful not to cramp.

For your thighs, slide your right leg a foot or two behind you, toes pointed, and contract the muscles on the front of your right leg and the right side of your butt. You should feel both very strongly. Flex those muscles hard for six seconds, and then do the same with your left leg.

Stand with your feet comfortably apart, as if you were going to press a heavy weight overhead, and flex your thigh and butt muscles. Hold for six seconds. To better feel this exercise, you can even raise your arms overhead, as if you really were pressing a heavy weight.

Place one leg at a time to the side, toes pointed sideways, and flex your thigh muscle.

For your hamstrings (the muscles on the back of your leg), stand normally, and then curl your right leg up behind you. You should feel a contraction in your hamstring. Go easy at first, as the hamstring muscle is easily pulled. As you gain strength, increase the intensity of your contraction and hold it strongly for six seconds. Do both legs.

With your hamstrings, you might find better leverage and a better feel in your muscles if you lean forward while curling your leg. Experiment and find what works best for you.

That completes your exercise routine.

Do your Jackknife Pushups three days a week, with a day of rest between workouts. Do your Chin-Ups twice a week. Do your flexing and tensing exercises every day. They only take a few minutes.

Breathe during all of your exercises. Exhale while exerting. With your Jackknife Pushups, breathe in as you lower your body and breathe out as you push your body up. When flexing, breathe out as you contract the muscle.

You want to finish your workouts feeling pumped, refreshed and energized, not worn out. If you push yourself to the point where your muscles are quivering and shaking, it's going to be very hard for them to recover. In fact, recovery from such a workout can take weeks. Most weight trainers push themselves to that point and end up in a state of chronic overtraining. As a result, they don't make any gains. Eventually, they quit training.

Train hard, yes. But don't overtrain.

The old-timers coined a saying for this: Train, don't strain.

Remember to get plenty of sleep and rest.

Remember to eat good, nutritious food, and try ingesting some protein within twenty minutes after finishing your workout. This can be as simple as a glass of raw milk, or it can be a complete meal.

The body thrives on regularity, so try to train around the same time every day. You don't *have* to do this, but it's beneficial if you can.

Along with regularity in your training, try to eat at the same time each day. And try going to bed at night and rising in the morning at the same time every day. Your body is going to love you.

If your current situation does not allow regularity, then do the best you can. You can build muscle on all kinds of wacky schedules. It's not easy, but it can be done. Above all, think positively. Dedicate yourself to success.

Advanced Chest and Back Training

After completing three to four months of Jackknife Pushups and Chin-Ups, your shoulders and arms will be considerably larger. You can continue the program just the way it is for another three to four months, or you can do some advanced training for your chest and back.

Switching from an emphasis on your shoulders and arms to an emphasis on your chest and back is easy. All it requires is two simple changes. First, switch from doing Jackknife Pushups to doing regular Pushups on the floor. This will focus the exercise on your chest muscles, and to a lesser degree on your triceps.

Second, switch from doing Chin-Ups with your palms facing you to doing Pull-Ups with your palms facing away from you and your hands wider than shoulder width apart. This change in grip will focus the exercise on your latissimus dorsi muscles. The latissimus dorsi—or lats, for short—is the wide sweeping muscle that extends from under your armpit to your waist. Nothing builds this muscle faster than Pull-Ups performed with a wide overhand grip.

Starting with Pushups, perform them in the same manner as your Jackknife Pushups, with two sets of five to six reps, and then slowly build up to four sets of twenty reps.

Use perfect form with your feet together, your back straight, and your eyes looking straight ahead. Tense your entire body, lower yourself all the way down until your lower chest touches the floor, and then press back up. The only thing that should move is your arms. Follow each set of Pushups with six seconds of flexing exercises for your chest.

When you are able to do four sets of twenty reps in the regular floor Pushup, you can increase the resistance by placing your feet on a small stool or chair for your last set. Start with five or six reps for that set with your feet elevated, and then build up, just like you did with your Jackknife Pushups.

For your Pull-Ups, space your hands wider than shoulder width apart and your palms facing away from you. You should feel an immediate stretch in your lat muscles. Pull up until the base of your neck touches the bar and then lower yourself down.

If you want, you can pull up until the back of your neck touches the bar. Either version will work.

Work up to two sets of six reps, and then up to three sets of eight reps. Flex your lats for six seconds after each set. Your upper body is going to grow very wide, very fast.

Leg Training

At this point, you might be wondering what exercises you should do for your legs. The flexing and tension exercises we discussed earlier for your thighs, hamstrings, and calves will do wonders for your legs. Throw in some running, sprints, and mile runs, and your legs are going to look and feel very muscular.

If you're looking for some additional leg work, try doing bodyweight squats, probably the simplest exercise in the world. Stand comfortably with your feet twelve to fifteen inches apart. Look straight ahead and keeping your heels flat on the floor, squat all the way down, and then rise up. You should feel the exercise in your thighs and butt.

Work up to one set of twenty reps, and then progress up to two sets of twenty reps. At that point, you're going to have a choice to make. You can either work up to one set of one hundred reps, or you can do a warm-up set of twenty reps, followed by one or two sets of one-legged squats, probably the most difficult exercise in the world.

To perform a one-legged squat, stand next to a chair or stool and place one hand on it to help you balance. Then raise one leg off the floor, point it straight ahead of you, and attempt to squat down on one leg. Don't be surprised if you fall to the floor. You can also try this exercise by standing on the seat of a chair—not a chair with wheels on it—placing your hand on the back of the chair, raising one leg, and squatting down. The exercise is actually easier to perform this way as your free leg can point below the level of the chair seat. That change in leverage decreases the resistance you have to push.

In either case, proceed with caution. This is a difficult exercise; one that could take you months to master. You might have to work up to quarter reps, then half reps, and only then complete full reps.

Once you are able to complete a full rep, work on completing a set of six reps. Anyone who can complete ten full reps of one-legged squats, all the way down and all the way up, is a monster.

I didn't include any form of squatting in your exercise routine earlier, because leg work can be taxing and most guys who start out in bodybuilding are interested in making fast gains on their chest, shoulders, and arms. Too much work will cut into your recovery time, so you might want to hold off on squats until after you complete at least one three month cycle on Jackknife Pushups and Chin-Ups.

I've always made my best progress when I performed one core exercise, followed by one assistance exercise, which is what you have with Jackknife Pushups and Chin-Ups. Whenever I added too many exercises, my progress slowed and dried up. Don't make the same mistake.

Extreme Cases

Every now and then I encounter someone who is so weak they have difficulty just holding the top position in a Jackknife Pushup. Others can barely grip a pull-up bar, and when they do, they can only hold their weight for one second.

Some of these people are cancer patients. Others are simply weak and out of shape. Many were born sickly (as I was), and have had numerous childhood illnesses (as I have). Their conditions were compounded by growing up in a household with abusive parents, parents that fought and bickered, and served nothing but junk food to eat (like my household). If that's the case with you, don't fret. I have the perfect solution.

Perform only the flexing and tension exercises and nothing else. Do them slowly, concentrating on the muscle you are working, and then hold the contraction for a full six seconds.

Do these exercises every day.

Practice flexing various muscles and then try moving your legs and arms, feeling your muscles tense and flex as you move them. You will soon discover some new, unique positions to hold. You'll be inventing your own exercises, which is always cool to do.

You can build a terrific body with nothing more than these flexing and tension exercises. In fact, there's a famous bodybuilder named Maxick who did just that. He was one of the strongest men in the world in his time and he built his body almost entirely with flexing and tension exercises.

Maxick called his exercise system Muscle Control, and even wrote a book with that same title. Some people claim that Maxick built his body with weights, but they are wrong.

He demonstrated his strength with weights; and prior to weightlifting competitions, he trained with weights in order to strengthen his tendons and master the necessary technique involved with each movement. But as he explains in great detail in his own book with his own words, he built his body with flexing and tension exercises.

The Naysayers Will Abound

As your muscles grow and people begin noticing, you're going to be approached by various individuals who will either comment on your physique or ask about the program you're following. Common questions include, "What are you doing for your shoulders?", "How did you get your arms so big?", or simply, "How much do you bench?"

Whether you choose to engage these people in conversation is up to you. In my case, if a person approaches me in a sincere way, I always answer their questions and I try to be as helpful as possible. There's a universal brotherhood among bodybuilders, and I do my best to continue that tradition.

If I suspect the questioner is not sincere, I smile and answer them politely, and then move on.

Mixed in among both the sincere and insincere questioners, will be many well-meaning, but confused individuals who, once they learn the kind of program you're following, will tell you that what you're doing is all wrong.

These folks have been brainwashed into believing that the only way to build muscle is with weights. If you tell them you're not using weights, they will react first with disbelief, and then with ridicule. They will also immediately insist that you drop what you're doing and start hitting the weights. Even people with little to no muscle at all will tell you this, which would be laughable if it weren't so sad.

The best way to deal with people like that is to smile and say, "Thanks," and then continue doing what you're doing. Sure, you could engage them in discussion, but you'll find it to be a waste of time. Trying to explain to someone who is hooked on weight training why bodyweight training is both safer and more effective is like talking to a wall. Believe me, I've been there and done that.

Many of them simply won't believe you when you tell them you don't lift weights. In their mind, it's impossible to build huge muscles without weights, and they will project that disbelief onto you. They will think you're lying to them.

If you encounter someone like this, don't get into an argument or a fight; it's just not worth it. Simply shrug and walk away.

Now if you decide to start training with weights at some point, that's up to you. I don't recommend it, but you have the right to do so. I will tell you this: There's nothing that drains your recovery time faster than lifting weights.

You can test this out for yourself.

Perform your normal 20 minute workout of Jackknife Push-ups, Chin-Ups, and flexing exercises. Note how you feel afterwards, and note how you feel an hour or two later. In most cases, you will be 80-90% recovered within a couple of hours.

Now rest a day or two and then perform a 20 minute workout with weights. Note how you feel afterwards, as well as how you feel an hour or two later. In most cases, you will feel tired and sluggish. You might even want to take a nap. That's the effect training with weights has on your recovery ability.

Lifting weights will drain your energy in other ways, as well. When you are forced to balance an external weight, such as a weighted barbell, it produces a strain throughout your entire central nervous system. That's debilitating.

Compound that with multiple sets done over multiple workouts and you're looking at a recipe for disaster.

There's a machine called a posturometer. It's a meter that measures posture, and it uses a numerical system to show how much tilt and rotation a person has in their spine. A rating of 7 or higher is considered extremely out of alignment. No one with a rating that high should be lifting anything heavy.

Now get this: Almost everyone who trains with weights has a posturometer rating of 10 or higher. In other words, their spines are severely out of alignment.

You might be familiar with the name John Madden. He's an ex-NFL head coach. In fact, he won a Super Bowl as the head coach of the Oakland Raiders. After he retired from coaching, Madden became a television broadcaster and regularly appeared on Monday Night Football.

One night, Madden made a very revealing comment. A player had just been injured and was being carted off the field. Madden's fellow broadcaster mentioned how muscular the player was and how he was always lifting weights.

Madden nodded and said that players who work out with weights the most are the first ones to get injured.

Martial artists have told me the same thing.

So think before you leap.

You can build a magnificent body without weights. You can do it fast and in complete safety. With weights you can do the same, but it will take longer and your body will be at risk of injury. Eventually, no matter how careful you are, your spine will go out of alignment.

No one has ever injured themselves or threw their spine out of alignment by doing Pushups or Chin-Ups. However, millions of people have injured themselves and thrown their spines out of alignment while lifting weights.

Bodybuilding, properly done, can transform your life. I can't recommend it more highly.

IMPORTANT NOTE: If you took the fake vaccine for the phony coronavirus, do not perform any of the exercises in this book, or any other form of exercise.

I hate to be the one to tell you that, but I have to, because doing so just might save your life.

Over four million people worldwide who took the jab have died and close to twenty million people who took it have been seriously injured. Most of the deaths have come from heart attacks, so you'll have to refrain from doing anything that puts a strain on your heart, such as exercise.

That also includes boxing, wrestling, and the other self-defense methods we discussed in the last chapter. Right now, MMA fighters who took the jab are dropping like flies. So are other athletes.

You'll probably have to avoid exercise for the rest of your life. Instead of exercise, you need to detox your body. I've written a book on the subject with some basic information in it. Detoxing is a long process, so the sooner you start the better.

It's not a hopeless situation. It's bleak, but it's not hopeless. Some dumbasses will tell you it's hopeless, but with God all things are possible. Toxicity is toxicity and all toxicity can be removed from the body over time.

It sucks, I know. Whoever encouraged you to take the jab is a scum-sucking liar who needs to be purged from your life. In fact, you may want to purge everyone from your life who took the jab or went around wearing a face diaper. They've shown you who they are.

They've shown you their cowardice and their willingness to bend their knee to tyrants.

They've shown you how fear and stupidity prevented them from researching any facts.

They've shown you how they surrendered their freedom and their country without a single shot being fired.

They've shown you how they chose hysteria over honesty.

They've shown you their supreme weakness of character and how they will betray you at a moment's notice

How can you expect loyalty from them ever again? How can you expect loyalty from people who are not loyal to themselves?

Purge them from your life.

Chapter Six

Why You Should *Never* Enlist in the Military

Don't enlist in the military. Don't *ever* enlist in the military. If you do, it will be the biggest mistake you ever make in your life. I know. I was duped into enlisting and it was the dumbest thing I ever did. I don't want you to make that same mistake.

There are four primary reasons why enlisting in the military would be the worst mistake you ever make in your life. Let's examine them one by one.

First, America is the Great Satan.

Did you know that?

Three quarters of the world call America the Great Satan.

They do that because the United States—not its citizens, but its government, its military, and its media—are exporting violence and sick perversion to every country they come in contact with.

That's why America is so hated and why the majority of the world refers to us as The Great Satan. The low opinion that our neighbors hold for America might change in the future, but it won't be in the *near* future. It will take decades, maybe even centuries, for America to undo the damage it's done around the world and lose its reputation as the Great Satan. That's not without reason when you consider that our government has done nothing but bomb and invade other countries for over 100 years.

If two World Wars in the 20th century weren't bad enough, here's a partial list of countries the United States has bombed, and in some cases invaded, since 1950. Call it the Democracy World Tour:

Korea 1950-1953
Guatemala 1954
Indonesia 1958
Cuba 1959-1961
Guatemala 1960
Congo 1964
Laos 1964-1973
Vietnam 1961-1973
Cambodia 1969-1970
Guatemala 1969
Grenada 1983
Lebanon 1983-1984
Libya 1986
El Salvador 1980s
Nicaragua 1980s
Iran 1987
Panama 1989
Iraq 1991-2003

Kuwait 1991
Somalia 1993
Bosnia 1994-1995
Sudan 1998
Afghanistan 1998
Yugoslavia 1999
Afghanistan 2001-2015
Yemen 2002
Iraq 2003-2015
Pakistan 2007-2015
Somalia 2007-2008, 2011
Yemen 2009, 2011
Libya 2011, 2015
Syria 2014-2015, 2017

Not a single one of those countries attacked the United States, but we sure attacked them. Not a single one of those countries harmed an American citizen or posed a threat to American lives. But we sure killed plenty of their citizens.

Not only that, but with every one of these countries, and with all of the countries we bombed during World War II, the United States deliberately targeted civilians rather than military targets.

That's a style of warfare our military has been following since the 1860s when General William Sherman, under the direct orders of President Abraham Lincoln, ran roughshod over the Southern states. Sherman's army murdered and raped women and children, burned down farms and cities, slaughtered horses and farm animals, and left no living thing alive, not even a blade of grass.

That method of warfare worked so well, our military has been following it ever since, targeting civilians, particularly children, and murdering them in the most horrific ways imaginable.

In World War II, the United States military, along with Britain, purposely firebombed the citizens of Dresden, German. Walt Whitman Rostow, a man who had never fought in a war or experienced actual combat himself, made the decision to firebomb Dresden, a non-military target. Rostow picked the city of Dresden to firebomb, because its citizens were predominantly Christians, and he picked February 13 and 14, 1945 as the days to do it, because February 14 fell on Ash Wednesday, a Christian holy day.

By ordering the firebombing of Dresden on Ash Wednesday as he did, Rostow intended to turn its Christian civilian population into ashes. That is exactly what happened. The heat on the ground at Dresden reached over 1,000 degrees and melted both people and asphalt. The Christian people of Dresden, over 35,000 of them, including thousands of children, were literally burned alive.

Rostow continued to pick civilian targets to bomb throughout World War II, and again in the Vietnam War, when he was an advisor to President Lyndon Johnson. Rostow called for the all-out bombing of North Vietnam, targeting as many civilians and children as possible.

Rostow died on February 13, 2003, the anniversary of the firebombing of Dresden. He's now in hell. The people he burned alive suffered a brief instant of horrifying pain before dying. Rostow is experiencing that same pain every second of every day for all eternity.

The firebombing of Dresden was not an isolated incident. Far from it. Less than a month later, on March 9 and 10, 1945, the United States military firebombed Tokyo, Japan, again targeting civilians and children, and killing over 100,000 people by burning them alive. It was the single most destructive bombing raid in history.

Then in August of 1945, the United States military atom-bombed Hiroshima and Nagasaki, Japan. (Some top-notch researchers say neither city was atom-bombed, but rather hit with a combination of napalm and mustard gas.) Both bombings were unnecessary as Japan had already offered to surrender, but President Harry Truman, a 33rd degree Freemason, ordered the bombings anyway. Hiroshima and Nagasaki were civilian targets with no military value and populated mainly by children.

Hiroshima was bombed first on August 6, 1945 and 80,000 people, mainly children, were instantly killed. Another 50,000 died later from wounds and sickness.

Apparently that wasn't enough, because only three days later, on August 9, 1945, the United States bombed the city of Nagasaki. This time 70,000 people were instantly killed, and thousands more died later from wounds and sickness.

Nagasaki was bombed for the same reason that Dresden was bombed—it was a non-military target, comprised mainly of children, and almost all of its citizens were Christians.

Nagasaki was so heavily populated with Christians it was known as the Japanese Vatican. The bombing of Nagasaki was deliberately detonated above the Urakami Cathedral.

That's what America does best—bomb civilians, kill as many children as possible, and murder Christians. That's literally all the United States military has done since World War I—bomb and invade other countries and kill civilians and children.

We did it all through World War II and all through the Vietnam War. We did it in Iraq, Syria, and Afghanistan. We've done it at one time or another to practically every country on earth. And then there's Russia and China.

As I type these words, the United States is fighting a proxy war with Russia, and threatening to go to war with China. A proxy war means the United States isn't doing the actual fighting—the Ukraine is—but the U.S. is supplying arms, ammunition, and money to the Ukraine in order to fight Russia. It's no different than you giving someone a gun and paying him ten thousand dollars in order to shoot a person you don't like. You're not the one pulling the trigger, but you're responsible for it.

The Ukraine wanted to surrender shortly after its military conflict with Russia started in order to save lives, but the United States refused to let them do that and ordered them to keep fighting.

Since then, over 200,000 lives have been lost fighting for the Ukraine and thousands more for Russia . . . all because the United States refused to let the Ukraine surrender.

At the same time, the United States government and the media are beating the drums for war with China, falsely claiming that the "pandemic" of 2020 to 2022 was caused by a Chinese lab leak. It's a colossal lie, but fat, dumb Americans believe it.

Is it any wonder why America and the United States government are so hated around the world?

All-in-all, over three fourths of the world's countries and people hate America. They don't hate you personally, but they hate the United States government, along with its military and its media for bombing and invading innocent countries, and for targeting civilians and children.

By the way, it's not just the children of other countries that America murders, they do it to the children of this country too. On April 19, 1993, the United States government attacked a peaceful religious community in Waco, Texas with flame-throwing tanks and burnt it to the ground, killing 76 people, including 23 children. The victims had done nothing wrong; they'd harmed no one and posed no threat to anyone. Yet our government burned them alive. Fat, dumb Americans watched it happen on television and then did nothing. They didn't even complain.

You would think that our military indiscriminately murdering millions of little children would produce at least a little remorse in those doing the killing. But that's not the case at all. They feel no remorse at all.

After our first war with Iraq in 1991—a war in which hundreds of thousands of children were deliberately targeted and killed—the United States imposed sanctions on that country, which then killed an additional 500,000 children. This was done after the war ended, making the sanctions completely meaningless and unnecessary.

Madeline Albright was our country's Secretary of State at the time and responsible for those sanctions. She was asked in 1996 how she felt about her part in the murder of 500,000 children. The question put to her was, "We have heard that half a million children have died. I mean, that is more children than died at Hiroshima. And, you know, is the price worth it?"

Albright replied, "I think that is a very hard choice, but the price, we think, the price is worth it."

You'll be happy to know that Albright is now dead. She's burning in hell and being tortured by demons, along with everyone else who's ever had a hand in the harm and murder of innocent children.

The Just War

Now there is such a thing as a just war—a war that's justified by acting in self-defense or to eradicate evil, such as the conquest of Mexico by Hernan Cortes. Cortes and his men were forced into war with the Aztec Indians in order to put an end to their barbaric practice of human sacrifice.

The problem with the United States is that we almost never engage in a just war. Quite the contrary. The United States has been the aggressor and the instigator in nearly every military conflict we've ever engaged in.

Our war against the Barbary pirates was a just war. The Muslim pirates of the Barbary States were attacking American ships, stealing their cargo, and selling captured American sailors into slavery.

The War of 1812 was another just war. Britain was seizing American ships and forcing American sailors to serve in the British Navy.

The Vietnam War began as a just war. It was an attempt to protect the people of South Vietnam and prevent the spread of Communism. But it quickly devolved into our nation's usual style of warfare—targeting civilians and murdering as many children as possible.

Those three wars are pretty much it. They're the only three times in our country's history in which we engaged in a just war.

There are plenty of fat, dumb Americans who will scream with outrage over that. They're the same ones who believe Germany started World War II and that the "pandemic" of 2020-22 was a real thing. They believe whatever they see on television and they don't know the truth about anything.

So that's reason number one why you should never enlist in the military. If you do, there's a good chance you'll be sent to fight in one of these illegitimate wars against an innocent country that hasn't attacked us, or in a war against our own citizens. In either case, you'll be forced to murder and bomb children and civilians. Even if you never see the battlefield, you'll still bear responsibility just for being part of the machine. You'll have the blood of those dead and wounded children on your hands. After all, that's how America fights its wars.

Sick Depravity to Go With Your Violence

The second reason why you should never enlist in the military is closely related to the first. Not only does the United States military export violence and destruction everywhere it goes, it also exports homosexuality and trannyism, with United States embassies flying the rainbow flag. That has probably contributed more to America being called the Great Satan than all of the children we kill.

Don't discount the power of flags. Flags are symbols of submission and allegiance. When you see U.S. Embassies flying the rainbow flag, what they are telling the world in clear, unmistakable language is that the United States submits and pledges allegiance to homosexuality, sodomy, sexual perversion, and the sexual mutilation of children.

It's telling the world that America celebrates as its highest value a sin that the Bible says cries out to Heaven for vengeance. And our message to other countries is to either accept homosexuality, trannyism, sexual perversion, and the sexual mutilation of children or we will bomb you.

Kay Griggs was a woman married to a Colonel in the United States Marine Corps. In a series of startling interviews, she detailed how the entire United States military high command is riddled with homosexuals, a virtual infestation, including almost every married officer, holding the rank of major or higher.

If that's true, it doesn't surprise me. In fact, it goes a long way in explaining both our country's continuous stream of battlefield defeats, as well as our military's penchant for bombing civilian targets, murdering children, and torturing P.O.W.s. If you enlist in the military, you will be serving under these sickos and making the world safe for sodomy.

The current military conflict between Russia and the Ukraine plays right into this. There are multiple geopolitical reasons for that conflict, but right alongside of them is the push by the United States to make every country on earth accept homosexuality, trannyism, and the sexual mutilation of children. When the United States illegally overthrew the government of the Ukraine in 2014, the first thing they did was start pushing homosexuality. Russia doesn't want that, but the Ukraine, under the control of the United States, insists on forcing it on them.

The third reason why you should never enlist in the military, and it's as good of a reason as the first two, is that everyone opposed to the brutal violence and corrupt morals that our military exports—in other words, everyone who's against bombing civilians, against torturing P.O.W.s, against homosexuality, against the murder and sexual mutilation of children—has been purged from the military. The good guys have all been kicked out and the only ones left are the sickos we just mentioned.

Those sickos are also incompetent. And in the military, incompetence will get you killed.

How incompetent are they, you ask? In 2021, we lost a war in Afghanistan to an army of goat herders. Not only that, but we lost in humiliating fashion with a cowardly retreat that made us the laughingstock of the entire world.

Interestingly enough, while the United States military is riddled with sick and perverted homosexual officers, the military men of Afghanistan that we lost that war to are uncompromising alpha males. That difference in masculinity may have played a bigger role in the defeat of the United States than incompetence.

I'm talking here about the officers and decision makers. Among the enlisted men, 99.9% of them have no idea what's going on. What's more, they don't care. The vast majority of enlisted men in the military are dumb to begin with. Add to that how enlistment standards have been drastically lowered and you're talking the dumbest of the dumb. That's who you'll be serving alongside of and it makes yet another reason why you should never enlist in the military.

If you do enlist, you'll be serving alongside some of the stupidest people on earth. Sure, you might meet one or two guys you can talk to; guys with some semblance of intelligence. But they will be few and far between. Most likely you'll be surrounded by morons, while taking orders from sick, perverted, and mentally twisted officers.

You'll have no privacy. You'll be surrounded day and night by dumbasses. If you have any intelligence at all, you'll start to go mad.

Forget the movies and television shows you've seen. They have no basis in reality and there's nothing heroic about serving in the military at all. Where's the heroism in bombing civilian targets, murdering children, and torturing P.O.W.s?

All of those movies and television shows you've seen are filled with lies and the actors starring in them are almost all homosexuals. I met most of them when I was in the movie business. With one notable exception, they're all flaming homos.

Don't throw your life away by basing it on a fictional character in a fictional movie portrayed by a homosexual actor. You'll regret it from the very first day that you arrive at boot camp. Only then it will be too late.

The closest representation to actual military life you'll ever see in a movie is the first hour of *Full Metal Jacket*. There you'll find an honest portrayal of boot camp in the Marine Corps. If anyone still wants to enlist after watching that movie, they are mentally ill with suicidal tendencies.

The final reason why you should never enlist in the military is because once you do, the government owns you. You're no longer a citizen with rights; you're a piece of property owned by someone else. They can literally force you against your will to do whatever they want, including injecting you with harmful and deadly "vaccines."

If the idea of being someone's slave with no mind of your own appeals to you, then go ahead and enlist. However, I can't imagine anyone who's intelligent enough to be reading this book having that mindset.

If you're white and thinking of enlisting in the military, you really need to have your head examined. As we've pointed out already in this book, the people running the country want you dead. Under their "leadership," the country has betrayed you and stabbed you in the back. You owe this country nothing.

Don't enlist in the military. Don't *ever* enlist in the military. If you do, it will be the biggest mistake you ever make in your life. I know, I've been there.

Heaven and Hell Revealed in War

Before we leave this chapter, there are four important items I want to discuss.

First, for more information on the firebombing of Dresden, you can watch a movie called *Hellstorm: The Untold Story of the Genocide of Germany.*

You can also read the book *Hellstorm: the Death of Nazi Germany 1944-1947* by Thomas Goodrich. Neither the book nor the movie are for the squeamish.

Second, I want to tell you about a miracle that occurred at the bombing of Hiroshima. As we already discussed, 80,000 people died instantly when the bombing occurred and another 50,000 died later from wounds. President Truman, a Freemason who is now in hell, boasted, "Man has learned to produce the power of the sun here on earth."

Among the only survivors of the Hiroshima bombing were four Jesuit priests, Hugo Lassalie, Hubert Schiffer, Wilhelm Klensorge, and Hubert Cieslik. They lived only eight blocks from ground zero where the bomb detonated. Everyone else within a square mile was killed, but these four men suffered only minor injuries. They were praying the Rosary at the exact time that the bomb hit and they credited the Rosary and the message of Our Lady of Fatima for their survival.

Not only that, but all four of these men lived for years afterwards. They were examined over 200 times and no trace of radiation or mustard gas poisoning was ever found on them. Their building also survived the blast; the only building for miles around that wasn't demolished from the blast.

If praying the Rosary can save four men from a major bombing that killed everyone else for miles around, don't you think you should start praying it?

Some Historical Truths

Earlier in the chapter, we talked about the concept of a just war and we used the conquest of Mexico by Hernan Cortes as an example of one. I'm willing to bet money that you were never taught the truth about Cortes and his heroic battle against the Aztec Indians. Were you or were you not taught in school that the Native Americans (Indians) that the early American explorers and settlers encountered were a noble race, mostly peaceful, who lived in harmony with nature and the environment until the white man showed up and stole all of their land, slaughtering them in the process?

If you weren't taught that, I'd be very surprised. But guess what? It's a pack of lies.

The truth is that with few exceptions, the Native Americans that the early European explorers encountered were a brutally violent people who murdered with impunity; worshipped serpent gods, and engaged in human sacrifice, cannibalism, sorcery, and witchcraft.

The Aztec Indians of what we now call Mexico sacrificed over 20,000 people a year, mainly children, and then ate their bodies. The sacrificial victims ranged from newborn babies to young teens. The ceremony the Aztecs practiced began with shrieks, whistles, and thunderous drumbeats as the doomed victims were dragged up the steps of the Aztec altar and held down on their backs over a stone slab.

It took four priests to hold the victim in place, one for each arm and leg. While the victim screamed, a fifth priest raised a jagged knife and plunged it deep into the child's chest. The priest tore out the still beating heart and held it aloft, gushing blood for the shrieking crowd to see. Then the priest cut off the child's head, legs, and arms. The heads were impaled on sticks, and the legs and arms were cooked and eaten. Young children were considered a particular delicacy. You were taught that in school, right?

The Aztecs slaughtered their victims by the thousands, one after the other, until the priests collapsed from exhaustion. They did this for centuries until the Spanish arrived and put a stop to it. The Aztecs were only one tribe out of hundreds that were just as bloody and barbaric as they were.

The American Plains Indian was no different. In some ways, they were even more brutal. They engaged in scalping, mutilating bodies, taking slaves, kidnapping children, raping women, both white and Indian, and torturing prisoners.

Time after time, the early European settlers were horrified by the violence, brutality, and depravity of Native Americans. The Spanish begged the Aztecs to give up their practice of human sacrifice and cannibalism, but the Indians refused.

You can read all about Native Americans in the books *Scalp Dance: Indian Warfare on the High Plains, 1865-1879* by Thomas Goodrich; *Cortes: The Great Adventurer and the Fate of Aztec Mexico* by Richard Lee Marks; *Saint Among Savages: The Life of Isaac Jogues* by Frances Talbot; *Saint in the Wilderness: The Story of Isaac Jogues, Missionary and Martyr in the New World* by Glenn D. Kittler.

If you prefer reading fiction, try the *The Searchers* by Alan Le May and *The Big Sky* by A. B. Guthrie, Jr.

These books are not for the squeamish. Their blood-soaked pages will turn your stomach. But if you want to know the truth about Native Americans and the violent struggles faced by the early American settlers, there it is. These books and others present a true picture by people who were actually there at the time and saw it firsthand.

Yes, it's true that the United States military was brutal to the Indians right back, killing as many women and children as possible, and slaughtering the buffalo that the Indians depended on for food. We addressed the actions of the United States military earlier in this chapter, but it doesn't change the fact that American Indians were a violent, bloodthirsty, and warlike people.

What you've been taught in school regarding Native Americans is just one lie your teachers have told you. I could provide you with hundreds of more examples. Basically, everything you've been taught in school about slavery, the Civil War, World War I, World War II, the Korean War, the Vietnam War, our country's elections and political processes and how it all works is nothing but lies.

Here's another one: I'll bet any amount of money you were taught in school that Germany started World War II.

Am I right? Is that what you were taught?

The reality is Poland, France, and Britain, with the urging of the United States, started World War II.

Sound crazy? It might, but only if you've been lied to by your teachers. Here's what really happened, which you can easily verify yourself with the aid of any honest history book.

Poland in 1939, under the dictatorship of Edward Rydz-Smigly, was brutally torturing and murdering German civilians in an area called the Danzig Corridor. Women were beaten, raped, and murdered. Men were castrated (had their balls cut off) and murdered.

Said William Joyce, who was there at the time and witnessed these atrocities firsthand, "German men and women were hunted like wild beasts through the streets of

Bromberg. When they were caught, they were mutilated and torn to pieces by the Polish mob . . . Every day the butchery increased . . . Thousands of Germans fled from their homes with nothing more than the clothes that they wore."

Germany appealed to Poland for months to stop these attacks, but Smigly refused. In fact, the attacks grew worse and Polish partisans crossed the border to attack a German radio station. Germany was finally forced to invade Poland in order to stop the murder and mutilation of its people.

Two days later, France and Britain declared war on Germany—Germany didn't declare war on them. A month later, France invaded Germany—Germany didn't invade France until much later.

Germany repelled the French invasion and spent the next several months pleading for peace with Britain and France, but both countries refused. That's how World War II started. Is this true history of how the war started the same history you were taught in school? If so, I'll eat my hat.

Perhaps you were told a half lie. Perhaps you were told the truth as I outlined it above, but with the smug addition that France and Britain had to declare war on Germany, because they had a treaty with Poland. That's a lie too, a lie of omission.

Yes, France and Britain had a treaty with Poland, but at the same time that Germany invaded Poland for the express purpose of saving the lives of its own citizens, Russia also invaded Poland in order to seize territory. France and Britain said nothing about Russia's invasion of Poland and they never declared war on them. They only declared war on Germany.

Were you taught in school about Lazar Kaganovich, the "Butcher of Ukraine"?

During the 1930s and 1940s, Lazar Kaganovich was singlehandedly responsible for murdering more people (over 20 million, almost all of them Christians) than any other person in history.

Kaganovich's organized gangs swept into a village, killed all the men, raped all the women, stole all the food, and then burned the village to the ground, leaving the women and children to die of starvation.

Kaganovich was responsible for the Katyn Massacre of World War II, in which 20,000 Polish officers and men were brutally murdered.

You can read about Kaganovich in the book *The Wolf of the Kremlin*, written by his nephew, Stuart Kahan.

That's quite an education you're getting at your school, isn't it? They're lying to you about the conquest of Mexico and the brutality of Native Americans, lying to you about World War II, and conveniently not telling you about the worst war criminal and mass murderer in history.

Why do you think that is?

Could it be because they're too busy shilling the phony election and baseless claims of global warming?

Chapter Seven

How to Attract Girls—and Why You Shouldn't

If you skipped ahead to this chapter without reading the preceding ones, then I can pretty much guarantee you're going to have trouble with women in your life.

How can I make such a bold statement? Easy. By skipping ahead to this chapter, you're demonstrating an unhealthy need on your part for the approval of women. You're placing women ahead of your own wellbeing. You're giving them an inordinate amount of attention and focus, when what you should be doing is concentrating on your own self-improvement. Doing so will put you much further ahead in life than chasing a skirt.

Attracting girls is easy and I'm going to show you how to do just that, but the more important issue is why—why on earth do you want to attract girls in the first place? The more desperate a person is to attract girls, the more out of touch they are with the female mind and with their own mind. That desperation is fueled by conflicting advice from people with no knowledge on the subject of just what it takes to attract girls in the first place.

Nothing that anyone has ever told you about women and how to attract them is based on rational thinking; rather it is all emotionally based, and because of that, it is factually wrong.

On one end of the spectrum you have well-meaning know-nothings telling you to just "be nice," which is useful only on the most superficial level.

On the other end are the wannabe pickup artists, who couldn't get a date to save their lives, telling you to act "alpha," with no idea of what that even means. They have no clue what they're talking about as evidenced by their dateless lives. And here's a tip: anyone who uses the word "alpha" in reference to attracting women is an idiot.

By the time you finish reading this chapter, you'll know exactly what it takes to attract girls and have them chasing after you, but you'll also be so disgusted with the female mind that you won't want anything to do with girls ever again. Curious? Keep reading.

In addition to women trouble, if you skipped ahead to this chapter, then I can pretty much also guarantee that you've bought into the myth of romantic love. Romantic love is a lie; a lie that continues to worm its way into contemporary life, because it benefits women at the expense of men. Don't fall for it.

Romantic love is the ridiculous belief that one day you will meet the girl of your dreams—your "soul mate"—and from that point on, life will be wonderful. Nothing could be further from the truth.

The myth of romantic love was dreamt up approximately three hundred years ago by rich snobs with too much time on their hands. Over the last 70-80 years, that same idea has been popularized by songs, movies, and television. The truth is romantic love does not exist.

Before the myth of romantic love began, people married when they were young, often around the age of thirteen or fourteen. Then they raised a family together.

If you're currently in middle school or high school, then the chances are good that if you had been born in an earlier generation, you'd be married right now and living at home with a girl your own age.

Take a look around you at the girls in your school and neighborhood. If you had been born 500 years ago, you'd be married to one of them right now, and it wouldn't be to the one you're salivating over, but to a girl that your parents or grandparents picked out for you—most likely that nerdy girl with glasses that you can't stand. You'd be married to her. How do you like them apples?

Perhaps you're breathing a sigh of relief. But perhaps you'd be happier today if you *were* married to that nerdy girl with glasses. When people married in earlier generations, those marriages lasted longer and worked better than marriages today and it had nothing to do with romantic love.

They were called arranged marriages, and neither the bride nor groom had any say in the matter. Some cultures still practice arranged marriages. And you want to know something? They work. Divorce among arranged marriages is almost non-existent. Families are more stable. Societies are more stable. That's all gone now.

Because romantic love is a myth, it would be a waste of time for you to pursue it. But romantic love is what society tells you to pursue, isn't it? Either that or you're told to have as much promiscuous sex as you can.

You can chase all the women you want, but don't be misled into believing that one day you're going to meet the perfect girl who's going to make your life wonderful and complete, or that you even need a girl to make your life wonderful and complete. Those are myths too.

Platonic friendships with females are another myth. In case you don't know, the word "platonic" comes from the Greek philosopher Plato. A platonic friendship means being friends with a member of the opposite sex, only without romance or sex. In other words, being best buddies with a girl, but not going any further.

That's yet another lie in a mountain of lies and it was spread in the same way that the myth of romantic love was spread, through movies, books, television, and music.

Men and women are so different in the way they think that platonic friendships are virtually impossible.

You can't be friends with a girl for any extended period of time without sex rearing its head. It simply cannot be done. One of you will always be thinking of getting it on with the other. If it's not you, it's her. And if it's not her, it's you.

Without the possibly of sex dangling before him like a carrot on a stick, no man can spend more than ten minutes in the presence of a girl without becoming bored out of his mind. Can you? If it wasn't for sex, most men wouldn't spend any time around women at all.

That's the reality.

Feminized men will say they don't mind being around women, and some of them claim they actually enjoy it. But that's a lie. The only reason they put up with women is because they're hoping it will lead to sex, something they haven't had in years or even decades. So they hide their simmering frustration beneath the surface and project an air of tolerance. But even soyboys have their limits.

If you think your situation is different, go ahead and try being friends with a girl. Only be sure to tell me how it works out. You don't even have to tell me; I already know how it will turn out. She'll string you along, you'll get bored and frustrated, and the whole thing will sputter to a halt.

Women will argue hysterically that platonic friendships are healthy and widespread. As usual, they are wrong.

The reason why women want you to buy into the myth of platonic friendships will become clear to you before you finish this chapter. See if you can figure it out before I explain it.

So where does that leave you?

Your parents are not going to arrange a marriage on your behalf, although there's no harm in asking.

Your father will laugh and give you a pat on the back, and your mother will faint.

With an arranged marriage out of the question, you're going to have to solve this woman thing on your own.

You want a girl that's pretty, obviously. But personality outshines looks.

You want a girl that believes in you and supports you. Someone who understands that a man is the head of the household. Don't get involved with anyone who doesn't believe that. In fact, it's a good idea to not get involved with any girl who doesn't fit into your long range plans of marriage. All you'd be doing is wasting both her time and yours.

So how do you meet a girl like that?

And how do you get such a girl to like you back?

To answer both questions, it helps to first understand what you're dealing with.

Women think differently than men.

Now there are plenty of dopes who disagree with that statement and insist that women and men think alike. But they are wrong about that just like they are wrong about everything else.

We're going to cover some of the different ways in which men and women think right now. I'll be speaking in generalities. Not all women and not all men are the way I'm about to describe, but the majority of them are. I think you're intelligent enough to understand that.

It's also worth noting that everything you're about to read here regarding women, also applies to feminized men. That shouldn't surprise you.

For the most part, I'll be discussing women over the age of sixteen. Most girls under the age of sixteen still possess some degree of innocence. Our modern education system has done everything it can to destroy that sense of innocence, but it hasn't completely succeeded. That sense of innocence is one of the reasons why men throughout history have always been attracted to young girls.

Are you ready to take a deep dive into the female mind?

If so, gird thy loins and soldier on.

A Deep Dive into the Female Mind

Women are the ultimate life distraction, the great man-killer, the torpedo that has sunk more men's ships than all of the German U-boats and submarines of World War II put together.

Women are born nation-wreckers, a role they have embraced throughout history. They instigate trouble within their own nation and then side with their nation's enemies.

Men will fight and die for their country, their faith, and their family. Very few women will do that. Because women are weaker than men and unable to defend themselves physically, they will jump ship to the winning side in any conflict, even if it means abandoning their own men and turning traitor on their own country.

If you find that extreme and are having a hard time believing that women would actually turn traitor so easily, look at the hundreds of examples that history has shown us. Better yet, look at society today and abortion. Millions of women over the last forty years alone have literally murdered their own children. For a woman who murders her own child, turning traitor on her own man and her own country and leaving them to die is nothing.

In fact, if you want to see evil up close and personal, visit or view images from a pro-murder (pro-abortion) rally. You'll see hundreds of unhinged, mentally ill women literally lusting for the legal right to murder their own children. Observe the self-loathing and demonic hatred spewing from their faces. Note also the handful of feminized men in attendance, desperately trying to ingratiate themselves with these baby-killers in the hope that it will lead to sex.

Through abortion, women have murdered more people than have died in all of the wars fought throughout history combined. And all of their victims have been their own innocent children.

By the way, don't think you're off the hook when it comes to abortion just because you're a man. Who do you think is making all of these women pregnant? If you impregnate a girl and she has an abortion which you failed to prevent, then you're just as guilty of murder as she is and you will suffer the same fate—burning for eternity in the fires of hell.

You can see women betraying their own men and their own country playing out right now in Europe, where millions of women are mating with "migrants," whom they perceive as representing the winning side in the current war against Christianity. European women can see that Christianity is losing so they have conveniently jumped ship to the other side, abandoning their own men in the process. Not only that, but European women were instrumental in creating and supporting the invasion of Europe in the first place.

This traitorous aspect of women is a survival mechanism. A man knows that if he loses a war he will most likely lose his life. But a woman knows if her country loses a war, her life might be spared, albeit as a sex slave. So the second she sees the war tilt one way or another, she aligns herself with the winning side. Thousands of years of doing that has hardwired such behavior into the female mind. Feminized men are no different. They, too, will turn traitor on their country and jump ship to the winning side.

Another way that the female mind differs from the male is in the way it perceives reality. There are two aspects to this. The first is that the average women cannot tell the difference between her feelings and reality. The average woman believes if she feels something then it must be true. This is a basic feminine characteristic. Because the average woman cannot distinguish the difference between her feelings and reality, the actions of the average woman often appear delusional or downright insane.

This creates an abundance of chaos in life, particularly in legal matters. Our entire legal system of courts and due process is designed for English-speaking men, using facts, evidence, and logic to determine the truth and deliver justice. When you insert women and feminized men into the mix, they immediately let their feelings dictate their reality, which results in confusion and chaos.

The second aspect to this concerns the difference in the way women and men analyze and critique new information. When a man encounters new information, he asks, "Is this true?" When a woman or a feminized man encounters new information, they ask, "What will people think of me if I think this is true?"

Read those last two sentences again. They explain a huge difference in the way men and women think. Because women and feminized men engage in group think—what will people think of me if I think this is true?—they automatically interpret new information according to whatever the group deems to be appropriate. In other words, whether the new information is true or not is irrelevant. What's relevant to them what other people say is appropriate.

Women literally need other people to tell them what to think. Truth is irrelevant. Logic is irrelevant. They will go along with whatever the herd agrees to go along with, no matter how ridiculous.

This goes back to the days when most people on earth lived in small communities or tribes and depended upon each other for survival. Everyone living in those close-knit communities was expected to play a necessary part. Troublemakers or those who refused to go along with the herd were kicked out in order to ensure survival of the group.

A rugged individualist could survive such an expulsion. Indeed, many did, taking to the wilderness and becoming mountain men who lived off the land. However, for a woman or feminized man to be ostracized from the herd was nothing less than a death sentence. In order to avoid that, they became adept at going along with whatever the herd was doing. Conformity for them became a survival tactic and it remains hardwired into their psyche.

Look at the mass hysteria displayed by women and feminized men during the "pandemic" of 2020-2022. That was conformity on steroids. And it followed the same pattern we've seen throughout history.

Robert Bartholomew, a sociologist in New Zealand who has collected data on over 800 outbreaks dating back to 1566, says that in 99 percent of mass hysteria events the majority of sufferers are female. *99 percent!*

Yet another way in which men and women think differently, is the way they perceive themselves in the world. Men see themselves in terms of their accomplishments and what they contribute to the world. Every man wants to be useful and known for contributing something beneficial to society.

Women see themselves in terms of their sexual value, and they base their decisions in life on whether or not the issue in question increases or decreases their sexual value. Because of that, women sexualize everything.

Have you ever wondered why women in both Europe and the United States support unfettered immigration?

Even though unchecked immigration destroys nations, Western women support it wholeheartedly, because it creates a huge influx of "migrant" men, who then compete with the nation's natural born male citizens for the attention of Western women, thus raising Western women's sexual value.

If the gender of "migrants" was reversed—if instead of millions of young men flooding a host country, it was millions of young women—the same Western women who support immigration so enthusiastically today would be out in the street tomorrow protesting against it.

That's because an influx of young women, competing with them for the attention of the host country's men, would immediately lower their sexual value.

This compulsion that women have to maintain and increase their sexual value creates a need for constant attention.

Look at the women in your life. What do they do all day? I'll tell you what they do, they click around on their phones, checking to see how many "likes" they got on their social media accounts and how many guys sent messages to them. Then they compare their results with those that other women received to see who has the highest sexual value. They're also out shopping or getting their hair and nails down in order to better sexualize their appearance and attract more attention from men.

Remember when we talked about platonic friendships with women? I told you that women become hysterical when someone points out to them that platonic friendships between men and women are impossible. Having read this far, can you guess why that is?

The answer lies in what we just discussed—a woman's need for constant attention and the importance she places on her sexual value.

A woman knows that any guy she's friends with is only hanging around because he's attracted to her sexually. Either that or he's gay. Otherwise, why would he be wasting so much time with her?

Women know this, but refuse to acknowledge it because having that male friend around fuels their need for constant attention and increases their sexual value.

Remember too that most women are unable to separate their feelings from reality. Even if she's ugly as sin and a woman that no man would ever engage with romantically, in her mind that guy who's hanging around and being her "friend" is sexually attracted to her. That explains why you often see older women ripped off by gigolos and con men.

Guilt and Self-Reflection

When a man does something wrong or hurts someone in any way, he feels intense guilt. In fact, it often haunts him for years. Many men lie awake at night feeling remorse for mistakes they made decades ago. Other men hide from their past through alcohol or drugs.

Women are not that way at all. They seldom, if ever, experience guilt or remorse for the past. Can you name one time a female in your life expressed guilt or remorse for something she did or someone she hurt in the past?

Read fiction written by women prior to 2023. You won't find a single scene of self-reflection in which a female character expresses guilt or remorse over her actions or for doing something that caused harm to others. The reason why you won't find such a scene is because the female authors themselves are incapable of such feelings. (If you know of a book containing such a scene, please tell me.)

Look at *Gone With the Wind*. It's 1,000 pages long, written by a woman, and not once does Scarlett O'Hara, the lead character, express even the slightest remorse for the consequences of her actions and the damage she's caused. Women love that book. They've made it a bestseller for decades. Now you know why: because Scarlett O'Hara is just like them; cold, callous, and unremorseful.

My two favorite female authors are Esther Forbes and S.E. Hinton. Yet even they do not include scenes of guilt or remorse among their female characters, and they write very few such scenes for their male characters.

In *Johnny Tremain*, written by Esther Forbes, the lead character of Johnny has some bad things happen to him. You feel bad for the guy and he feels some pity for himself, which is understandable. But there isn't a single scene in the book that I can recall in which he feels any type of guilt or remorse. There's certainly no such scene involving any of the female characters.

In S.E. Hinton's three major books, *The Outsiders*, *Rumble Fish*, and *That Was Then, This is Now*, you won't find a single scene in which a female character experiences guilt or remorse for her actions.

In *The Outsiders*, the character of Johnny feels guilt over killing a guy in self-defense, but that's it.

In *That Was Then, This Is Now*, the lead character betrays his best friend for life and sends him to prison—and feels no remorse over it. And he does it because of a girl!

Only a female writer could compose a book like that, because only a female is that incapable of feeling remorse for her actions.

What Women Look for in Men

What do all women have in common when it comes to romance? What are they all looking for in a man?

The answer is status.

Some people refer to status as fame, but it's actually more than that. Women *are* attracted to fame—to actors, musicians, athletes, etc. However, fame is only one of the many ways in which status is reflected.

Status refers to a person's place in society. The more elevated a man is in society, the more women become attracted to him, regardless of his age, looks, or any other factor. That's why a blond bimbo in her twenties will marry a billionaire in his eighties. It's not so much the money, but the status that money reflects and that money can buy.

As men, we couldn't care less about a girl's status. We don't care whether she's a janitor, a waitress, or a CEO. All we care about are two things: is she nice and is she good-looking? And if she's super nice and makes us feel special, we can cut her some slack on her looks. That's literally all men care about.

With women it's entirely different. They pay some attention to looks, but it pales in comparison to the attention they pay to status. As for being nice, they hate it. They don't want men to be nice which is why you should never, ever give flowers to a girl, or act nice in any unusual way.

A women's interest in status goes back to what we discussed earlier regarding the herd mentality of the female mind. A woman won't think or believe anything until others tell her what to think or believe.

You can see this reflected through things like fashion, books, etc. Women change fashions constantly because the people who make and sell those fashions tell them to. If they were left on their own, women wouldn't do this, but when they see everyone else around them dressing in a new and different way, they immediately imitate it.

Things such as bestseller lists for books exist for the same reason. Women and feminized men won't buy or read a book unless and until they see that everyone else is buying or reading it.

This is called "social proof." Whatever other people approve of, women and feminized men become instantly attracted to. Not because the thing or the person that others approve of actually deserves the approval, but because everyone seems to think they do.

It's monkey-see, monkey-do behavior, and women are the monkeys.

Remember what we talked about earlier? When women and feminized men encounter new information, they don't ask, "Is it true?" They ask, "What will people think of me if I think this is true?"

That's what social proof is. It's why so-called pickup artists will show up at a bar or nightclub with an attractive woman on their arm, a woman actually hired to play that part. Other women see that and immediately assume that the man has status, because he was able to attract the woman on his arm. That makes the man much more attractive to them than if he were to show up at the bar or nightclub alone.

In terms of fame and sexual interest, women will immediately salivate over whatever celebrity the mass of humanity has singled out for status. Knowing this, you can turn any man into a sex symbol merely by giving him a significant place of status.

Thus, a music producer can take five skinny, feminine-acting male teens, turn them into a musical group, and project them into the public eye, knowing that women will immediately fawn all over them.

Sadly, other young men see that and assume they have to look skinny and act feminine in order to attract girls too. When it doesn't work, they have no idea why.

This herd behavior on the part of women leads them to lust after every celebrity imaginable. However, despite their desperation to mate with such high-status men, most women don't have access to them. Therefore, they will look to the men in their life that best reflect high status. This can often lead to bizarre and unusual situations, such as a woman's sexual attraction to killers and gangsters.

You might find what I'm about to say next absolutely revolting. It's certainly revolting to me, but here it is: when a serial killer or a guy who has just murdered his wife and kids is arrested, he's immediately flooded with love letters from women. Not just one or two letters, but hundreds of them, many containing marriage proposals.

Now if you figure that each letter-writer represents a hundred or more other women who feel the same way, but don't have the time, the courage, or the opportunity to send their own letter, you're looking at literally tens of thousands of women who are sexually attracted to serial killers and to men who murder their own wife and kids. Think about that. Guy brutally murders his wife and kids, kills them in cold blood with no remorse, and women around the world are suddenly turned on and want to have sex with him.

These aren't grimy old whores sending those letters either. Some of them are, but the majority of the letters are written by young, pretty girls—the same girls that young men are trying to woo with flowers, candy, and poems. It would be laughable if it weren't so tragic.

The attraction that women have for serial killers and wife-murderers is triggered by status. Women see these men paraded across television and the female mind interprets that as high status. There's also the taboo factor.

Because these men have killed and murdered innocent people—acts considered taboo by civilized society—it triggers something primitive in the female mind. It makes the man different and on a higher level of status than any other man in her life. So she dreams about marrying the guy and sends him love letters.

As a young man, all you want is a cute girl who laughs at your jokes and treats you nice. And yet an extremely large segment of those very same girls that you're eyeing as potential romantic partners are lusting after serial killers and men who just murdered their wives and children. Others are lusting after celebrities. Some are lusting after each other. It's literal insanity. It's the female mind.

How to Attract Girls Without Even Trying

Let me relate to you how this dynamic has played out in my own life. Within it, you'll discover the secret to attracting girls. That is, if you still want to.

There have been four times in my life when women have made themselves openly available to me without my having to lift a finger. One second I was standing alone, without a romantic prospect in sight, and the next I was deluged by girls wanting to fool around with me. They came out of the woodwork with no effort on my part at all. The common denominator in all four of those experiences was a sudden rise in status on my part.

When I was sixteen-years-old, my parents kicked me out of the house and told me never to come back. Penniless and living on the street, I talked myself into a job with a traveling carnival, eventually operating a ride called The Zoomer.

That was in Ohio and in every city and little town we traveled to I had girls aged fourteen to nineteen interested in me romantically.

141

Where do you think that romantic interest came from?

If you think it came from status, you are correct. But what kind of status? I was literally homeless with thirty cents in my pocket. Everything I owned fit inside a paper bag. At night I slept under the stars or in the cab of a truck.

The reason I received an avalanche of romantic interest was because when these girls saw me operating a carnival ride worth tens of thousands of dollars, they decided I must be a person of status. No other boy they knew was doing that.

Remember, very few women have access to the high-status celebrities and serial killers they lust over. All they can choose from are the men available in their immediate life.

By nature of the job I held, even though the pay was pitiful, I was a cut above every other boy in their small town. I was also an exotic stranger to them, thus elevating my status even more.

Finally there was the atmosphere of the carnival itself, with its bright lights and promises of fun and romance.

Put all that together and I had a new girl in every town we visited, sometimes more than one girl in a town.

Now I'm not suggesting you run off and join a carnival. I'm merely relating this incident so you can better understand how to attract girls yourself.

The second time I was flooded with romantic interest came when I was seventeen and eighteen-years-old. A movie came out that was a huge, blockbuster hit and I happened to look exactly like the star of the movie.

It was similar to my experience with the carnival in that I did virtually nothing to attract female attention, yet there it was. Girls flocked to me, wanting romance.

It was absolutely bizarre in that it had nothing to do with who I was as a person, and everything to do with the fact that I reminded them of someone else, who for that moment in time was the most desired male on the planet.

He was desired because he was the star of the most popular movie in the world, which gave him the highest status of anyone alive.

I was desired because I looked like him. In the warped mind of the female, that gave me status. They could kiss me and pretend they were kissing the actual guy who starred in the movie. I know that sounds retarded, but that's how the female mind works. Celebrity lookalikes tell me this is common.

Girls assumed that I had status, because I looked like someone that they regarded as having extremely high status. Because I looked like someone that other females around the world wanted to be with, they wanted to be with me.

My third experience with women making themselves available to me occurred as an adult. I became an actor myself, and after a long period of struggle, I landed a starring role in a movie. It wasn't *the* starring role, but it was a lead part and I received fifth billing among the cast.

There were about thirty girls, ranging in age from 18-25, on the set of that movie. Almost all of them, from the makeup assistant to actresses in the cast, made it very obvious that they were romantically interested in me. But get this—not one of those same girls would have given me the time of day if they'd passed me on the street the week before. The only reason they were interested in me now was because I had a part in a movie.

143

Prior to making that movie, I'd had a long dateless dry spell. Now suddenly I had girls throwing themselves at me. Why?

I was the exact same person. I looked the same. I talked the same. The only difference was a week ago I was unemployed, two months behind in my rent, and able to afford only one small meal a day, and now I was starring in a movie.

I had a conversation with one of those girls between takes on the set. She was twenty-one-years-old and she said to me, "You must have a lot of girlfriends, huh?"

"Why do you say that?" I asked her.

"Because you're an actor."

"What does that have to do with it?"

"Girls like guys who are actors."

I remember that conversation well, because it was the exact moment when I lost all respect for women. I realized that the attraction all of these women felt for me wasn't because of my looks or my personality or because I'd been nice to them, or for any reason other than in their minds I now had status. It had nothing to do with me as a person. If you'd have taken me off that movie and replaced me with someone else, all of those girls would have felt the same way about him as they did about me.

Later, when the movie was released, it happened all over again: a floodgate of female interest.

One girl cooed to me, "You looked so handsome in the movie."

No, I didn't. That girl worked in a sandwich shop a block from Venice Beach. I was a weekly customer there for two years and she never gave me the time of day. Now suddenly I was handsome? She only felt that way, because she saw me on a screen and I now had status in her mind.

Here's my final story of women making themselves available to me without my having to do anything. For five years I was the lead supervisor and night manager of a call center that was staffed primarily with women ranging in age from 18 to 29.

Similar to my experience with the movie, I suddenly had dozens of young pretty girls who let me know they were interested in me in obvious ways.

Some of them passed me notes with their phone numbers written down and told me to call them. One of those notes came from a cute 20-year-old who said she was in love with me. Other girls, more coy, asked me what I was doing that night after work and suggested they come over to watch a movie. Still others simply walked into my office, closed the door, and propositioned me. This went on all the time.

Whenever a girl quit or was fired, her replacement repeated the exact same behavior. I was like an Arabian sheik with my own private harem, and just as sinful, I'm ashamed to admit.

Once again, none of this had anything to do with my looks or my personality. It had nothing to do with my being "alpha" or any other such nonsense. It was due entirely to the position of status I now held. Prior to my being promoted to the position of lead supervisor and night manager, I was on the phone talking to customers just the girls. During that time, I received a few flirtations and subtle signs of interest, but it was nothing compared to the romantic attention I received after I became their boss. At that point the floodgates opened.

These were low income girls, living in low income areas, and I was now the highest status male that they had access to. That's where their interest stemmed from.

Do You Really Want a Girlfriend?

So we've come a long way in this chapter. You now know the secret to attracting girls without even trying. All you need to do is acquire status in their eyes. But before going on, I have to ask: do you really want to do that?

Knowing what you now know about the depravity of the female mind, do you really want a girlfriend? At this point in time, I don't.

What's more, it wasn't clear to me earlier in my life, but I now know that sex outside of marriage is a serious sin. I engaged in that sin a lot earlier in my life and now I spend every day regretting it and praying for forgiveness.

I didn't have anyone in my life offering me useful advice. Everyone I encountered was as clueless, or worse, as I was. I didn't have a book like this to show me how the world works. By having this book in your possession, you are miles ahead of where I was when I was your age. Only that's offset by how much more sinful and depraved the world has become.

Women were bad when I was growing up, but they're a hundred times worse now, particularly white women, and it has put a tremendous strain on men. Men today are working ten times harder than their grandfathers did in order to attract women who are worth twenty times less than their grandmothers. It's called hoeflation.

Add to that the sense of entitlement and vindictiveness among women today and the situation has become so intolerable that many men have abandoned women completely. They've either chosen to live celibate lives, or they've passed over white women in favor of more traditional and feminine Asian and Hispanic women.

I'm not recommending that. I've come to believe that race-mixing is wrong and should be avoided. But that's what a lot of men are doing. And I understand where they're coming from. Before I became aware of all the negative factors involved with race-mixing, I fooled around with girls of other races. And I found that they were all nicer, easier to get along with, and more feminine than liberal white women.

So I get all that. Only I didn't know then what I know now, which is that race-mixing leads to societal collapse.

History has shown us that every time a society engages in race-mixing it deteriorates rapidly. The most recent example is Europe. European countries like Germany, France, England, Sweden, Finland, Ireland, and others have all collapsed. They were stabbed in the back by their own traitorous leaders who drowned their countries with hordes of "migrant" invaders and encouraged race-mixing.

Low-IQ white women in Europe saw how the invaders were presented by the media and government as having high status (remember my experience as the exotic stranger?) and immediately took the bait, abandoning their native men. They also abandoned Christianity and reverted back to paganism. This has led to the collapse of the entire continent.

In Europe today, crime is rampant, the streets are littered with trash, people have no heat in the harsh winter cold, and thousands of women are being brutally beaten and raped every month by the migrant invaders, which quite frankly is what some (not all) of those women wanted.

The collapse of Europe is not an accident. It's intentional. And the primary reason behind it is the planned extinction of Christianity and the white race.

The scum-sucking president of France in 2008, Nicolas Sarkozy, gave a speech on December 17, 2008, at the Ecole Polytechnique in Palaiseau, France and said, "The goal is to meet the challenge of racial interbreeding: the Racial interbreeding that faces us in the 21st century. It is not a choice, it's an obligation, it is imperative. We cannot do otherwise. . . . If this volunteerism does not work, the State should move to more coercive methods."

In other words, we're going to collapse the country and eliminate white people by race-mixing, and if you don't go along with our plan we'll do it by force by importing huge numbers of rape-prone men from other races.

The same thing is now happening here. Race-mixing is winding its way through the United States, with low-IQ white women in America taking the bait, just like their sisters did in Europe. They've abandoned white men, abandoned Christianity, and are now engaging in every form of sexual perversion imaginable.

Just as these women have done, every major institution and corporation in America has also expressed their hatred and contempt for white men. As a result, many men have pulled back and said, "You hate us? You don't want us around? Fine. Just watch what happens when we're not here to keep the entire system running."

They've since pulled back from society and the result has been runaway inflation, food shortages, police brutality, train derailments, toxic chemical spills, infrastructure crumbling, corporate incompetence, humiliating military defeats, and rampant crime all across the country. America is collapsing before our eyes. And as more white men drop out of society, the situation will only get worse.

Diversity is not a strength, it's a weakness. Unity is strength. That's why race-mixing is so heavily pushed today. It's a deliberate effort to weaken and collapse the country.

How YOU Can Gain Status in the World

Now that you've had a look into the ugliness of female behavior and the female mind, I'll show you some ways in which you can attract women, that is, if you still want to.

First and foremost though, I want you to stay with girls of your own race. Don't engage in race-mixing. I know there are pretty girls of other races. I understand the attraction. But nothing good ever comes out of race-mixing.

So stick with your own race.

Next, I don't want you to engage in sex outside of marriage. That means you have to either remain celibate or seek out an appropriate girl to marry. You might find that advice frustrating, but if you stick to it, you'll thank me as you grow older.

To find an appropriate girl to marry, you'll have to attract her first. Let's talk about how to do that.

In order to attract girls, think about ways in which you can position yourself as a person of status in their eyes.

Competence is a form of status. It demonstrates that you are better than others at performing a particular task or skill. Knowing that, let girls see you doing something you're good at. It doesn't even matter what that something is. As long as you're good at it, they will notice.

At the same time, seek to become competent in skills that will benefit you. Learning how to spin a basketball on one finger is something very few people can do, but what good is it?

You could say the same thing about practically all sports. Unless you're good enough to earn a scholarship or turn professional, how is being proficient at sports going to benefit you in life?

Some exceptions are swimming, wrestling, boxing, martial arts . . . those are sports that might one day save your life.

At your age the only benefit there is to participating in sports, outside of earning a scholarship, is the status it will grant you in the eyes of girls. If you have no other options of achieving status, sports might be a way to go. However, you might have other options you haven't considered. Keep your eyes open.

If you're looking for a summer or afterschool job, look for something unusual that will give you a level of status. From seventh grade through ninth grade, I worked as a janitor at my school. That job contributed nothing to my status. But when I was sixteen and got that job running rides with the carnival, I had my pick of girls.

Are there jobs in your area that guys your age aren't doing, but that you could do well at it?

One job that will give you instant status is teaching. I don't mean teaching in the way that the lowlife teachers at your school are doing it. But rather teaching a skill or subject that people want to learn. The fact that you know how to do something that others are eager to learn, puts you in a high status position.

You don't need a school to teach, you can do it privately. Also, I would never suggest that you pursue teaching school for a living, because the world of academia is riddled with retards, perverts, and Communists, but if there's a skill you're proficient at or some sort of knowledge that you understand better than anyone else, there might be an opportunity for you to teach it.

If your school will let you teach or tutor students in the grades underneath yours, I guarantee you will have girls from those classes interested in you. You will be the highest status male in their lives.

In fact, if you can think of a way—any way—to interact with or be seen by girls a year or two younger than you, they will automatically grant you a level of status for no reason other than your being slightly older than them. You will appear different and exotic and they will be interested in you. Camp counseling is one such option.

Where do the girls you want to meet hang out? When I was in my twenties I worked in a vintage clothes shop a block away from Venice Beach. The beach attracted a boatload of girls, and because the shop I worked in was considered hip and trendy, it brought a lot of those girls inside.

I didn't enjoy the same kind of success with women there that I did with other jobs, but I did meet some girls. There was a girl in cutoffs that used to visit me at the shop where I worked who ended up moving to Hawaii. I still think about her every day and would give anything to see her again.

See if you can get a job or somehow put yourself in close proximity to an area ripe with female prospects.

You may have to think outside the box. But that's okay. Being different is a form of status.

When you see a girl you like, don't be afraid to say hi or to initiate a conversation. Just keep it casual.

Smile. Be friendly. Use appropriate humor. Learn their name and use it (people like when others use their name).

However you go about it once you meet a girl and she seems interested in you, ask her if she wants to hang out. Use those exact words "hang out." Don't say "date" and never ask a girl on a date. Never ask a girl to go to the movies, to dinner, or to a dance. Only ask her if she wants to hang out, and then arrange something casual: a walk, a drive, a shared activity. Think free and casual. If there's something you're good at, invite her to come and watch.

If you really want to impress a girl, take some classes in public speaking and join the debate team at your school. Then, when your presentation is polished, invite her to one of your debates.

Nothing demonstrates strength, courage, and confidence better than a smooth public speaker.

Public speaking is also one of the rarest and most sought-after skills a person can possess. It will brand you a winner and contribute immensely to the quality of your life.

Act like a man when you're with a girl. In other words, don't do anything stupid. Don't act immature. Use proper etiquette. Open the door for her. If you walk with her on the sidewalk, walk on the outside, closest to the street. If you're on a bus, train, or plane, sit on the outside, closest to the aisle.

At some point as you're hanging out, you'll have to make a move, either by taking her hand or kissing her. Don't wait for her to do it or you'll be waiting forever. Pick a moment that seems appropriate, like when the two of you are alone and she's standing close to you. If she's standing extremely close to you, leaning on you, or walking so close to you that her arm is brushing against yours, that's a sign that she wants you to make a move. Like everything else, keep it cool and casual.

If she rejects your move—at your age she probably won't, but if she does—don't worry about it. It happens to the best of us. Brush it off and separate yourself from her as quickly as possible.

Be polite. Say something like, "Thanks for coming with me. It was fun. I have to get home now."

If she doesn't reject your move, you're in business.

Don't brag to others about your success with girls or what happened when you were with them. You're better off keeping all that stuff to yourself.

If you hear other guys bragging about what they've done with girls, realize that fifty percent or more of what they're telling you is simply not true. But don't call them on it. Let them have their fun. In the same way that fishermen like telling tall tales about the size and length of the fish they've caught, guys like to brag about what they've accomplished with women. Just don't participate in it yourself.

Warning Signs of Women

Before you even approach a girl as a potential romantic prospect, there are things you should watch for.

If the girl you like has dyed her hair red, pink, purple, blue, orange, or green, be careful. Dyed hair is a sign of low intelligence.

If she has tattoos, be even more careful. Tattoos are a sign of even lower intelligence.

If she has both dyed hair *and* tattoos, be exceedingly careful. She likely has very low intelligence. Still, the main thing you want is someone who's nice and respectful. If she treats you nice, you can overlook her dyed hair and tattoos. I've dated girls with tattoos, and one of the most intelligent girls I've talked to recently was a black girl with tattoos on her neck, working as a security guard. There are always exceptions. But exceptions prove the rule, don't they?

If the girl you like smokes cigarettes, drinks alcohol, or uses drugs, I advise you to forget about her. She won't give up those filthy habits without a fight and in the meantime, you'll have to put up with it.

If the girl you like is into celebrities, and tells you how much she likes this one or that one, then cut your losses and get out quick. Celebrity worship is a sign of low intelligence and mental derangement. Note: this is going to knock out 98% of the girls you will ever meet in your life. You can hang out casually with someone like that, but don't harbor any illusions of a serious relationship. You'll be endlessly competing with fantasy images in her mind—a competition you'll never win.

If the girl you like says she's a feminist or that she supports abortion, BLM, homosexuality, trannyism, or any other form of woke leftist ideology you need to terminate the relationship immediately. You don't have to be rude about it, and you don't have to do or say anything that hurts her feelings, but you do need to forget about any potential romance. Those are all instant deal-breakers.

In fact, I advise you to purge everyone from your life who supports any of those things, whether male or female. Anyone who supports the murder of unborn babies, homosexuality, trannyism, lawlessness, rioting, or looting is on their way to hell. Why in the world would you want to be friends or spend time with someone like that? Just being around such a person is putting your own soul at risk of eternal damnation. Purge such people from your life and do it quickly.

Now if the girl you like is simply too pretty to pass up, and if you think you might be able to change her mind about any of those things, then maybe you can keep some sort of contact with her. But be careful.

Most young people have opinions about things that they really know nothing about. If a girl tells you she's a feminist, she might be repeating an opinion she heard someone else express, or she could be saying that because she thinks it's expected of her. Low-IQ adults do that too. They repeat whatever they see on television or hear on the radio and think it's their own opinion.

So if she says she's a feminist, but she doesn't really understand what that means and is unaware of feminism's Communist origins (feminism was created by the Communist Party in order to subjugate and enslave women, while simultaneously destroying the family unit), you might be able to get somewhere with her. You might actually be able to sustain a relationship with her and turn her into a sensible human being.

So if that's your motivation . . . to try and educate a girl and change her for the better, you can certainly try. However, your chances of succeeding are slim.

By and large, you're better off leaving the feminists, the celebrity chasers, and the baby-killers to the soyboys. They need love too.

To find out where a girl stands on these various issues, you'll have to feel her out (mentally, not physically). If one of these subjects come up in conversation, say to her, "What do you think about that?"

If the two of you pass a little kid on the street, say to her, "I like kids. I don't believe in abortion at all." And then listen to what she says. If she lays some feminist rap on you, make up an excuse and get out of there quick. You don't want to be around anyone, male or female, who enjoys murdering babies.

If she agrees with you, if she says she also like kids and is against abortion, you have a live prospect.

If the girl you like took the fake vaccine for the phony virus, and you should ask her early on if she did, you should probably forget about any potential romance. The fake vaccine isn't a vaccine at all, it's a gene therapy injection with deadly side effects and those side effects include "shedding," which can cause extreme harm to anyone in close proximity to them. Just standing next to someone like that could endanger your health and even your life.

If she took the jab she could also drop dead at any time. If that happens while she's driving and you're a passenger, you could both die. If she drops dead while the two of you are together, you could get blamed for it. Thousands of parents have been sent to prison after their babies died from vaccines. The media and medical establishment, lying like they always do, falsely claimed that the parent "shook the baby to death." Who is to say you won't be charged with murder like those parents if the girl you're with suddenly drops dead and there are no witnesses other than yourself?

Even if she doesn't die, she might suffer a massive heart attack or stroke, as so many other young people have who took the jab.

Now there's an issue of sympathy here. Most girls your age who took the jab did so because they were forced to do it by their brain-dead parents. Others were brainwashed by their idiot teachers and lying family doctors. If that's the case with your girl, you might want to cut her some slack.

Personally, if I met a girl who was exceedingly nice, cute to look at, and treated me well, and who happened to be brainwashed into taking the jab, I might continue to pursue a romantic relationship with her, provided she realized the mistake she made and took steps to detoxify her body.

On the other hand, if she became defensive and refused to acknowledge that what she did was wrong, if she refused to acknowledge science, I'd likely get out of there quick. I'd bail out for all of the reasons we've already discussed, but also because if I had children with her, she'd insist on giving them all of the deadly shots that cause autism, brain damage, and death. It would be one fight after another living with someone like that.

Tally Up Your Men

We've spent the majority of this chapter ragging on women. To be fair, let's turn to men. Almost all men today are feminized and they don't even know it. You can spot this quite easily. Here's how:

One of man's natural roles is that of protector, particularly a protector of women and children. There isn't a man on earth who seeing a woman or child attacked, doesn't feel an instinctual urge to protect them. Men take their role of protector very seriously. In fact, in the old days when a ship was going down, women and children were allowed to board the lifeboats first. When the Titanic sunk, it was mostly men who drowned. The lifeboats were filled with women.

Knowing that one of man's primary roles is that of protecting women and children, it becomes obvious that anyone opposed to that role—anyone opposed to men being able to protect women and children—is also someone opposed to masculinity and certainly not in possession of masculine energy. Since femininity is the opposite of masculinity, a person in opposition to the masculine role of protecting women and children must by logical extension be a feminized person.

Therefore, it's plain to see that any man who supports gun control in any form is feminized. Only a feminized man lacking in masculinity would deny other men the right to defend themselves and their families. These men are so feminized that their own instinctual urge to protect women and children has been short-circuited. That's what an abundance of brainwashing and feminism will do.

A man who supports gun control is so lacking in masculinity and so devoid of his own instinctual masculine urges that he fears he can no longer live up to his role as a protector of women and children. That fear causes him to want to bring all men down to his level by denying them the means of serving as protectors.

One of woman's natural roles is that of nurturer and mother. That doesn't mean that every woman should be a mother, only that every woman is designed to be one. Men, being the protectors of women and children, honor the role of women as nurturers and mothers.

Applying the same logic that we just used in terms of gun control, only a feminized man would seek to undermine a woman's role as nurturer and mother.

Therefore, any man who supports abortion in any way is feminized. No man, possessed of natural masculinity, would allow a woman to murder her own child.

In addition to their role as protectors of women and children, men are also protectors and governors of society. Therefore, every decision men make must be balanced with that in mind. Knowing that unfettered immigration creates crime, a destabilization of society, and lowered wages for the home country, men are naturally opposed to it.

Any man who is not opposed to immigration has relinquished his role as a protector and governor of society and is therefore feminized. He feels no allegiance to his country and no need to put himself at risk defending it.

We spoke earlier of how when faced with new information, a man's natural reaction is to ask, "Is this true?" While women ask, "What will others think of me if I think this is true?"

This makes women susceptible to brainwashing and to bullying by mass consensus. If the mainstream media tells them something is true, and every website they visit tells them something is true, and all of their friends tell them something is true, they will automatically accept it as true, not because it is, but because everyone else has accepted it. Therefore, if they believe it, they will be safe within the herd, whereas if they question or deny it, they could be subject to scrutiny, ridicule, and exclusion. In many cases, they are neither for nor against any particular issue, but will shift to whichever side is most popular. That is the feminine way of analyzing information.

Therefore, any man who accepts what he sees on television and the mainstream media without question and without performing any research of his own as to the accuracy of that information is feminized.

I could list over a hundred more ways of documenting real men vs. feminized men, but let's stick with these four. Apply them to all of the adult men in your life, particularly your teachers and school officials. Do they support gun control? Do they support abortion under any circumstances? Do they support immigration? Do they question what they see on television and the mass media and ask, "Is this true?", or do they assume it is true, because everyone is saying it? Do they believe in baseless conspiracy theories like fair and honest elections, the phony pandemic, and people are all the same?

I think you'll be shocked by the results.

I think you're going to find that just about every adult male in your life is feminized to one degree or another and that most of them are feminized to a large degree.

Feminized men are not a hopeless case. They can redeem themselves and become masculine males. All they have to do is change their thinking, which will then result in a change of behavior. Unfortunately, almost none of them are willing to do that. They're so far gone mentally, so utterly brainwashed, that they are never coming back to reality.

As this chapter has made clear to you, the vast majority of adults in the world today, both men and women, are only one step away from the loony bin. Don't become one of them.

God First, Girls Second

Girls are not the be-all and end-all of your existence. Keep in mind that throughout history more men have been ruined and destroyed by women than for all other reasons combined.

You're living in a world where women compete endlessly for attention in order to increase their sexual value. Don't get caught up in their web of deceit.

As a man, your primary focus should be honoring God. After that, it should be working, creating, and building.

That's your job, so to speak. You're here to be a creator. You're here to protect and care for women and children. In other words, you're here to be a man.

Modern society has turned this upside down. They don't want you to be a man. They want you to be a consumer.

Men are builders and achievers, not consumers. Your life does not revolve around the latest iPhone, the newest car, the coolest video game, the hippest fashion, or anything at all that emanates from the cesspool known as Hollywood.

Leave consumerism to the soyboys.

You're here to honor God, and to perform meaningful work.

Everything good and noble and useful in the world was created by men, just like you.

Every great battle of history in every just war was fought by men, just like you.

Every instance of good triumphing over evil was achieved by men, just like you.

Know who you are. And then act accordingly.

Remember, too, that if you're white the people that run the world want you dead and buried. And one of the ways they further that agenda is by promoting feminism and inserting a constant wedge between you and your chances of marrying and raising a white family.

They are relentless in their pursuit of your destruction, so you have to be just as relentless in thwarting them.

Put God first and make Him the focus of your life. Put your work second. Put girls a distant third.

Chapter Eight

Wealth, Money, Power! How Men Do It

What is wealth? Most people would define wealth as money. But money is merely a medium of exchange and the paper money we currently use to buy things is essentially worthless as it's no longer backed by gold or silver. (Our monetary system, which became totally corrupt with the creation of the Federal Reserve in 1913, is the biggest scam in the world. Anyone who tells you differently, including your teachers and college professors, is a fool, a liar, or both.)

Even gold and silver can become worthless. After Hernan Cortes and his men overthrew the diabolically evil Aztec empire, they were showered with gold as a thank you gift from neighboring tribes. The Spaniards began shipping the gold back to their own country, but each time they unloaded a shipment in Spain, it caused the price of gold to go down, and the price for food and other essentials to go up.

Meanwhile, the English who found very little gold in the northeast territories of North America that they claimed began shipping back to their native country fish, lumber, furs and other essentials. In a very short time, England overtook Spain as the world's most powerful country.

The gold that Spain was shipping back became essentially worthless, while the useful commodities that the English were shipping back contributed to the growth of their empire.

So what is wealth?

Some people say health is wealth. They have a stronger case than those who say that money is wealth. After all, what good is money if you're too sick to enjoy it? Yet people sacrifice their health for money every hour of every day.

There are lots of extremely rich people who have died unnecessarily from simple diseases like cancer that could have been easily cured for little or no money, but they lacked the knowledge of how to do that.

That begs the question: Can wealth be defined as knowledge? It can, and it makes more sense in the long run to value knowledge as wealth rather than money. Give me a choice and I'll take a wealth of knowledge over a wealth of money. The former can help you acquire the latter, but not the other way around.

Then there are people who define wealth in terms of close relationships with friends and family members. That sounds great on the surface and it makes some sense, but it's still a bit flimsy. We'll discuss that in a moment.

Finally, there are those who define wealth as spiritual wealth. I'm one of them. What good is all the money in the world, or the best of health, or all of the world's knowledge, or an abundance of wonderful relationships if you end up burning in hell for all eternity?

When you think of it in those terms, spiritual wealth is the only wealth that really matters. Yet very few people are pursuing it.

Back to those who believe wealth can be measured in terms of close ties with family and friends. The reason I said that outlook is a bit flimsy is because your family and friends won't be with you on Judgment Day. You'll have to answer to God for your sins alone. That makes your relationships here on earth transitory to the extreme. The road to Heaven is a solitary journey. It's basically every man for himself.

Now if your family and friends are assisting you on that journey, they can be wonderful assets. If they're praying for you now and will pray for you after your death, then they could possibly help you get to Heaven. Just be watchful for negative influences. There are plenty of people pushing all kinds of false knowledge and false religions.

As you can see, there are different thoughts on just what wealth is. I've made my position clear. To me, spiritual wealth is the only type worth pursuing. Having said all that, I know that many of you who are reading this book are looking specifically for tips and advice on making money. So let's talk about that.

The First Principle of Money

One of life's basic laws is you can't get something from nothing; you can't get without giving. So in order to get, you have to first give. You can always give something, even if it's only a smile. In order to make money honestly and consistently, one must provide something of equal or better value first. That something can be either a product or a service. That's the first principle of money.

At this point, you might be thinking of all the times you've seen people get without giving. It happens. We've all seen it countless time, both in business and on the street. But those who take without giving first are committing a great sin; a sin they will eventually pay for either here on earth or in the afterlife.

I used to give motivational talks to people living in low income neighborhoods and one of the first things I stressed was the concept of giving first in order to receive. Well, that part of my speech always went over like a lead balloon.

I gave hundreds of those talks and almost no one who heard them was ever interested in giving before receiving. What they wanted to know was how much they could take without giving.

And take they did. Almost all of them were living on some form of government assistance—food stamps, welfare, EBT cards, free phones, you name it. And when it came time to vote, the ones who bothered to do so, voted for whatever politician promised to give them more free stuff. That was their sole criteria.

The few people who paid attention to my talks and discovered ways in which they could give before receiving did very well financially. While the majority who rejected that advice remained in poverty and are still in poverty today. The more they took without giving, the poorer they became.

Now obviously, if you're crippled or otherwise unable to work, then surviving on government aid is acceptable. After all, what else can you do? But anyone who is able to work, but doesn't, and instead collects government aid for doing nothing at all is despicable. Such people are a cancer on society. They produce nothing of value, while taking from those who do. Today, tens of millions of able-bodied people living in the United States do just that. They sit at home, watching television and getting high, while living on the taxes that you pay

Others hold non-essential jobs as paper-pushers and project managers, contributing absolutely nothing to society. It seems like over half of the population in the United States is paid and rewarded for doing nothing at all.

Giving before getting is God's way of living. First, you plant the seed, then you till the soil (that's the giving part), and only after you do all that do you reap the harvest (the getting part).

When you give in order to receive, do it cheerfully, knowing that you are providing a product or service that benefits others. This is where a lot of people slip up. They're vaguely aware of the concept of giving before receiving, but they're not interested in benefiting others first.

The service or product they're offering is merely a cover—something of no real value, like the useless trinkets and beads the early American settlers offered to the Indians in exchange for gold and land, or like the cheap plastic junk we see for sale in shops all over America.

Businesses and governments do this too. In America today, almost every business in existence and the entirety of our government has forgotten the concept of giving before receiving. Their object isn't to make a good product that benefits the customer (giving before receiving), it's to make as much money as possible (taking without giving). Can you see the difference?

The Second Principle of Money

The second principle of money is best described through the following quote.

Whatsoever thy hand findeth to do, do it with thy might; for there is no work, nor device, nor knowledge, nor wisdom in the grave, whither thou goest.—Ecclesiastes 9:10

What that means is to work hard at whatever you do, whether that's shoveling snow, cutting grass, running your own business, or designing and building bridges . . . do it with all your might.

That doesn't mean moving at full speed twenty-four hours a day and wearing yourself out. It means showing up early, doing the best you can, and taking pride in what you're producing. It also means being thankful that God has given you an opportunity to turn your work into money.

A lot of people don't have that opportunity. Others do have it, but refuse to make the most of it. Rather than doing their work with all their might, they keep one eye on the clock and do their work as lazily as possible.

With certain low-level, stress-inducing jobs, where the boss is a slave driver out to exploit his employees for all he can, that type of slacker attitude is understandable. But most jobs aren't like that. If yours is, look for something else.

One of the keys to doing your work with all your might is finding your niche. Your niche is something in life that you can do better than anyone else on earth. If you're lucky or extremely talented, there are several things in life that you can do better than anyone else on earth. The trick is discovering them.

In addition to your niche, the thing that you can do better than anyone else on earth, there are things you can do which might not place you among the best in the world, but in which you are certainly in the top ten percent, or maybe even the top five percent.

Make it your mission to find out where your talents lie and what your niche is.

Sometimes talents appear early in life and sometimes they appear later. And sometimes you have to give your talents up for God. I've known since a young age that I could write better than most people. Today, I don't consider myself the best in the world at it, but I do know that I'm in the top five or ten percent.

I didn't know that I had any acting talent until I was in my twenties. Now there I do consider myself among the best in the world. There are specific character types that I can play better than anyone else alive. But when I discovered the truth about the movie business—it's a rotten, filthy business run and populated by rotten, filthy people—I had to give up acting for God.

You can see how that is a direct contradiction to what everyone else has ever told you about life, which is to "follow your dreams." But if I took that idiot advice, I'd follow my dreams straight to hell. That's because the movie business is run by outright devil worshippers. I'm not exaggerating when I say that. I mean it literally. In the same way that you and I worship God, they worship the devil.

They molest, rape, and murder children. They practice and promote rampant homosexuality. They're the most vile and disgustingly evil people imaginable. Yet the "follow your dreams" crowd would have me consorting with those people and helping to put money in their pockets.

"But it's your dream," they say, "your talent." True, but what good is talent and the fame that talent can generate if I end up burning in hell for all eternity?

When I tell people I gave up acting for God, they look at me like I'm crazy. Especially people who have seen me act. But you see, they're all mired in the material world. To them, fame, money, and the ability to sleep with an unlimited number of women is simply too good to pass up. They think there must be more to the story than what I'm telling them. But no, there isn't. I gave up acting for God. I'm more concerned with where I'm going after I leave this world than with anything the world has to offer.

I'm one of the top-5 professional football handicappers in the world, but I gave that up for God too. After the professional sports leagues all came out in support of the rioters and looters of 2019 and 2020, after they all came out in support of homosexuality and trannyism with their pride nights and pink jerseys and cleats, after they came out in support of the phony pandemic and forced their players and coaches to take the deadly jab, what choice did I have?

It was either give up football for God or risk going to hell myself. The decision was painful but obvious.

That's enough about me and my skills and talents. What are yours? What can you do better than most people and possibly better than anyone else in the world?

If you don't know where your talents lie just yet, relax. It will come to you as you get older.

Try different things. Experiment. Ask yourself what you like doing more than anything else. Your talents will reveal themselves.

Doing your best—doing whatsoever thy hand findeth to do with all thy might—is the second principle when it comes to money. The third principle is productive enterprise.

The Third Principle of Money

In an ideal world, men would earn their livelihood through productive enterprise—producing products or services that other people need or want.

That's how life used to be and how honest men used to make their living. It's certainly a factor that contributed to the wellbeing and happiness of Christian Europe that we discussed earlier.

Productive enterprise creates a win/win situation. Someone labors and receives compensation for producing something of value, while someone else receives the benefit of the product or service they purchased. Everyone wins.

In addition to that, such a system makes quality the competitive and determining factor. Everything from clothes to furniture is made with quality and built to last.

People engaged in productive enterprise take pride in their work. For men, this is an essential component to self-esteem. All men want to feel important and useful. Producing products of quality and workmanship is a way for men to achieve that.

Work, when focused on productive enterprise, is a healthy and character-building endeavor for everyone. Men who own their own company or farm, or work for someone who does, benefit tremendously by such work, along with the customers who purchase their products.

Today, fewer and fewer people are producing products or services that other people need or want. Instead, they are focused strictly on profit and how much money they can make. Nobody takes pride in their work and why should they? They're not being judged by the quality of their work.

Quality has gone out the window, and that's why everything you buy today falls apart after six months, why it's all cheap, shoddy junk. Even worse, more people than ever today have abandoned productive enterprise entirely and instead focus on speculation.

Speculation is making money for money's sake. In speculation, nothing is produced or sold. It's using money to make money, through stocks, bonds, interest, etc. Notice here how the first principal of money is being completely ignored. Nothing is first being given in order to receive.

In speculation, since nothing is produced, one party benefits (the party that makes money), while another party loses (the party that suffers loss in the exchange). Compare that to productive enterprise in which all parties benefit.

While speculation of this sort is legal throughout the world, it's condemned in the Bible. The Bible calls the practice of charging interest on money and loans usury.

If you remember the story of Jesus fastening a whip out of cords and driving the money changers out of the temple, that was because they were charging interest—usury—on the people. It's the only instance in the Bible where Jesus displays outright physical hostility. Knowing that, are you sure you want to engage in speculation and usury?

I'm not going to do it. I refuse to participate in usury in any shape, way, or form. Even with the money I keep in the bank. I have it in an interest-free checking account.

If God condemns usury and says it's wrong, then I don't want any part of it. I'm committed to living my life according to God's laws, not man's laws. And I'm certainly not interested in doing the same thing that every low-IQ moron in the world is doing.

Speculation is rampant in society today. And people do make money at it. But what good is that money going to do them when they die and go to hell?

My advice to you is to engage in the three principles of money: to give before getting, to do your work with all your might, and to practice productive enterprise.

In terms of things that people need and want and which they will happily pay money for, what comes to your mind?

Clothing is one such item. If you can produce high quality cotton clothing at a reasonable price, something no one in the world is doing right now (it's impossible to find 100% cotton socks), you will be in position to make a lot of money.

How about air conditioning? People need it and want it. If you could produce an inexpensive portable air conditioner, you could make millions of dollars and have fun doing so.

Let your mind do a little thinking. Ask yourself what people need and want, and then combine your answers with your own particular skills and talents. Million dollar ideas are right at your fingertips.

Should YOU Become Rich?

Now that you know the three principals of money, the burning question for you is should you become rich? Actually, I don't recommend it. The Bible speaks of how hard it is for a rich man to enter Heaven. Basically, a man cannot serve two masters. You can serve God or you can serve money, which also includes fame, social status, women, etc. Which do you choose?

Every rich person I've ever met, and I've met quite a few, is either on their way to hell or already there. Conversely, I've known a lot of poor people and based on what I observed of how they lived their lives, I'm convinced they are in Heaven.

Now you might be thinking that you can become rich in order to use your money to help others. That's a noble attitude, but here's the thing: other than Benjamin Freedman, a millionaire in the early 20th century and the author of the book *Facts are Facts*, I don't know of a single rich person in all of history that's ever done that.

Everyone who starts out with that goal in mind, who says they're going to make a lot of money and then use that money to help other people, never does. Before they're even halfway to their goal of becoming a multimillionaire, they've forgotten all about helping anyone else. Instead they've become solely focused on making more and more money.

There are plenty of rich people in history who *claimed* they used their money to help other people, and plenty of rich people today who claim the same thing, but guess what? They're all liars. If you look at where their money went and the so-called charities they donated to, you'll see that far from helping other people or making the world a better place, they did just the opposite. Their money lined the pockets of frauds, hucksters, and charlatans, and contributed to making the world a worse place.

You're going to meet people like that in life. Maybe you'll find yourself working for them, or maybe they'll be friends of yours who struck it rich. Without exception, they will sell you on the power of money and how they use their money to help this organization or that organization; or how they create jobs; or how their money benefits society. They're all delusional.

The fact is they're greedy. They're obsessed with making more and more money, and they justify their actions by giving away pittances here and there. Watch, observe the people in your life and you'll see that I'm right.

Money is a drug. It affects people's minds in ways you cannot even imagine. Judas betrayed Jesus for thirty pieces of silver. Other men have killed for a nickel. I have several friends right now who are literally paving their way to hell through their own greed and avarice.

Have you ever seen a riot? Look at the greed etched across the faces of the looters. They're stealing today and on their way to hell tomorrow, all because they couldn't resist stealing a pair of shoes, a case of beer, or a bottle of whiskey. In some cases, stealing all three.

You'll see that same look of greed on the faces of businessmen as they plot their next move. You'll see it on the faces of women as they compete for the attention of high status men. You'll see it on the faces of anyone who spends their time pursuing fame.

In this chapter I've given you the key to riches, and I've also suggested you try to avoid becoming rich. I want you to be financially comfortable, and if you decide to raise a family then I want you to have the means to do so. But I don't want you to be so heavily focused on money that you lose your eternal salvation. It would be better for you to remain poor your entire life, yet make it to Heaven, than to be rich your entire life and not make it to Heaven. No rich person I know has ever made it to Heaven.

Save Your Money

Spending money is easy—anyone can do it. What separates men from boys is saving money. Every time you earn a dollar—every time that money is fresh in your hands—keep it, don't spend it.

This one habit is going to put you so far ahead of the pack you'll never want to go back.

The first way this habit puts you ahead of everyone else is by giving you a cushion of finance that others don't have. The reason they don't have it is because almost everyone you're going to meet for the rest of your life spends their money as quickly as they get it, or even before they get it. They save very little, if any. Then on top of that, they borrow money and end up in debt that takes them years to repay.

Don't make that same mistake. Save as much money as you can and avoid debt like the plague.

How much of your income should you save? The ideal is 80%. Save 80% of what you earn and live off 20%. For adults, that's difficult. For a teen still living at home, it should be easy.

The second way that saving money will put you ahead of the herd is that once you begin the habit of saving 80% of your income and living off 20% (or as close to that as possible), opportunities you never imagined will open up, almost like magic. Perhaps a business idea that requires capital which you would not have had if you had not been saving money. Watch and see.

The more you learn about the world, the easier it becomes to save money. When you see just how corrupt and evil almost every corporation operating in America actually is, you say to yourself, "I'm not giving those bastards a dime of my money." At least that's the way it's supposed to work. The sad fact is most Americans are clueless about the world and how the money they spend contributes to the moral rot of society. Walk into any mall or shopping center in America and you'll see scores of low-IQ women spending obscene amounts of money on clothes, makeup, jewelry, and other wasteful items.

Not to be outdone, visit any professional sports arena in the country and you'll see thousands of low-IQ men spending hundreds of dollars on tickets, jerseys, beer, and concessions. A lot of these people—the low-IQ women in the shopping malls and the low-IQ men in the sports arenas—are married to each other. Stupid attracts stupid.

When it comes to girls, never spend more than five dollars on an outing unless and until you're married. That means no movies, no dinner dates, no nothing. If she doesn't like it, find another girl.

By the way, you're going to find living frugally and saving money to be a terrific litmus test when it comes to women. If the girl you're seeing is upset because you refuse to spend more than five dollars when you're with her, then that's exactly the kind of girl you don't want to marry or spend time with.

If you do marry her, she will proceed to spend all of your money, plus all of her own money and bury both of you in a mountain of debt. Then she'll leave you for another man.

On the other hand, if she's cool with you spending less than five dollars when you're with her and she understands your desire to save money, then that is a girl you definitely want to spend more time with.

If she, like you, spends as little of her money as possible while saving the rest, then she just might be the type of girl with whom you could build a life together and raise a family with.

So what can you do with a girl for five dollars? You can buy her an ice cream cone. You can buy two tickets to the Tilt-a-Whirl ride or the Ferris Wheel at your local carnival. That's about it, but that's okay. The best form of "dating" isn't really dating at all, as we already discussed.

Never buy a girl flowers or any other type of expensive gift. Never, ever, ever. I don't care how pretty you think she is. Don't do it. It's a waste of money and it will blow up right in your face.

In her eyes, you'll be a "soft touch" and any respect she had for you previously will be gone.

Ditch Your Debt

Debt equals death. Never forget that.

In French, the word "mortgage," which is the name given to the debt a person incurs when they borrow money to buy a house, means an agreement until death.

Pay cash whenever you can and don't get into credit card debt. Don't borrow money from your friends, don't borrow money from your family, don't borrow money from a bank or loan shark (banks are legal loan sharks), don't borrow money from anyone at any time for any reason.

This is some of the most important advice you'll ever get in your life. Don't take out a car loan, don't take out a business loan, and don't ever, EVER take out a student loan—it's the biggest racket in the world. If some smooth-talking teacher or school counselor tries to talk you into taking out a student loan, don't walk away, run away.

That teacher or counselor is probably getting a kickback. They have no qualms about saddling you with a lifetime of debt in order to receive their commission. Remember what we said about greed and how money affects people's minds? This is a prime example.

Neither a Borrower nor a Lender Be

By the same token, never lend money to anyone for any reason. Because you won't get it back. That I guarantee you.

Sure, the person who is asking you for a loan will swear up and down they'll pay you back. Don't believe it for a second, not even if their intentions are good and they believe they will pay you back. I'm telling you with 100% certainty you're not getting your money back.

If someone asks you to lend them some money, simply shrug, smile, and say, "Sorry." Then walk away. You don't have to explain anything else.

Now if you want to *give* someone money, that's different. I've given money to homeless people and others, but I knew it was a gift. I knew I wasn't ever going to get the money back.

Never sign an agreement or contract without reading and understanding every word. Never, ever, ever. That includes any agreement that you click on the internet.

Almost every contract you'll ever read—and throughout your life, you'll encounter dozens, possibly hundreds—contains clauses written in deliberately confusing language that's designed to take advantage of you one way or another.

You have to read and understand every word, and even then I would caution you about signing it.

Now eventually you're going to move out of the family house and rent an apartment (though I would recommend you continue living rent-free at mom and dad's place for as long as you possibly can, while saving your money). You'll also open a bank account. Those contracts are pretty straight forward, but still read them carefully.

With anything else, watch out. You could sign a contract to buy a car and end up paying thousands of dollars more then you thought you were paying.

The same thing could happen if you sign a contract for a smart phone or internet service. In fact, I would advise you to never sign any agreement that hits you with a monthly charge or takes an electronic debit from your bank account on a regular basis.

You have to be careful. Everyone is out to dip their grubby little hands into your pocket and extract a piece of what you worked for. To them it's business.

If you're a creative artist, someone who writes books, songs, or whatever, don't sign anything that gives away your rights to someone else. I can't tell you how many times I was approached by shysters, hucksters, and liars calling themselves producers, some of them working for major studios, who attempted to get me to sign away the rights to various screenplays and movie projects I developed.

If your school has a class in contract law, take it.

If you plan on traveling you'll need a credit card if you want to stay at a hotel. Get one with no annual fee and a limit of two thousand dollars or less. Use it only when travelling or buying over the internet. If you don't plan to travel, don't be in a hurry to get a credit card. If you do get a card, pay it off in full immediately every month.

Don't confuse living frugally or being thrifty with being a miser. A thrifty person is one who makes the most of what they have. They enjoy saving money and they make a game out of it. They tend to be happy people, and they are willing to share what they know and have with others.

Misers are the exact opposite.

The word "miser" comes from the word "miserable." Misers are miserable people who create misery for everyone else around them. Every interaction they have with others is one of taking, not giving.

Misers haggle over every price they see and browbeat shop owners into selling their merchandise as cheaply as possible. They're swindlers who take advantage of any opportunity to steal another person's money or property or to cheat them out of something that is rightfully theirs.

Misers are horrible, disgusting people who are never satisfied with what they have. They pay their employees as little as possible—minimum wage if they can get away with it—and they almost never give their employees raises.

Surprisingly, or maybe not, most misers are multi-millionaires and multi-billionaires. The people who run the world today are all multi-billionaires and they are all misers. They're not satisfied with what they already have—they want to take what's yours too. They want everything and they're very happy to start wars, create famines, and force jab people with poison in order to do that.

They're very happy watching other people starve to death while they enjoy sumptuous meals of steak, lobster, and caviar. At this moment, they're pushing the world to eat bugs. (For the record, if some fat, pink-haired Communist teacher tries to talk you into eating bugs, tell her what she can do with them.)

The mindset of a miser is rooted in scarcity—the belief that there's not enough to go around for everyone. That's why misers want to keep everything for themselves and leave nothing for anybody else. Unlike thrifty people who are willing to share what they have and know, misers keep everything for themselves and they refuse to share anything they have or know. Misers are suffering from a form of mental illness.

Quick Tips in Closing

Before we end this chapter, here are some quick money-saving tips.

Outside of a broken bone or a gunshot wound, avoid all doctors. They're quacks and charlatans. Don't give them a penny.

Don't pay for cable television or streaming services. You shouldn't be watching television anyway.

Don't pay for insurance, it's another scam and a fraud.

Don't join a gym. You can build a marvelous body without weights and machines.

Don't get your hair cut so often. It looks good long and you'll save money.

Take advantage of your local library and read books for free.

If you make a game out of saving money, it can be a lot of fun. And once you see your savings start to grow, it becomes even more fun.

Chapter Nine

Homeschooling is Best

Your life would be a hundred times better if you stopped attending school immediately and began homeschooling. The main reason for that is because your teachers are all lying to you.

Are they pushing the lie that hair-sniffing Joe won the 2020 election?

Are they claiming without evidence that the Stupid-19 virus was a real thing?

Are they spreading the widely-debunked conspiracy theory that Osama bin Laden orchestrated 9/11?

Well, guess what? They're lying to you.

Even worse, your brain-dead classmates are buying those lies. Some of them, anyway. There might be a few mentally sharp students at your school who know what's going on in the world. But knowing people the way I do, I seriously doubt it.

If your teachers are pushing any of the lies outlined above, and I'll bet $100 that they are, then you would benefit tremendously by choosing to homeschool.

Lies are like cockroaches, there's never just one. If your teachers are lying to you about the stolen election, the phony pandemic, or 9/11, what else are they lying to you about? Probably everything. And if that's the case, what kind of an education are you getting? It sounds to me like you're being indoctrinated, not educated.

You're not only being lied to at school, you have sick and twisted teachers acting as groomers and trying to indoctrinate you and your classmates into homosexuality and trannyism. Talk about disgusting.

What advantages are you receiving by remaining in school? Can you name one? Unless you enjoy listening to teachers who aren't qualified to clean a horse stable, much less teach a class, tell one lie after another, what possible benefit are you deriving from continuing to attend school?

You say you like school because there are girls there that you like to look at? That sounds like something a soyboy would say. There are girls everywhere. If you're willing to sacrifice your education, your mental stability, and your future all for the opportunity to catch a glimpse of some slutty, low-IQ girl with dyed hair and tattoos, then this book hasn't done you any good at all.

In fact, I would make the case that one of the best reasons to leave your school immediately is to avoid such girls and to avoid all idiots in general.

Idiot—noun plural, a stupid person

One of your primary missions in life is avoiding the company of idiots. That means just about every adult in your life, starting with your teachers, as well as the greatest source of idiocy on the planet—the idiot box itself—television.

Referring to others as idiots may sound harsh to you, but what else would you call someone who chooses to ignore facts and evidence, who refuses to accept reality, who believes every lie they see on television no matter how ridiculous, who surrenders their freedom in exchange for temporary comfort, who displays no empathy for others, and whose actions are directly responsible for the collapse and overthrow of the country?

When you look at it in those terms, the word "idiot" is actually quite mild. If you saw someone douse themselves with gasoline and set themselves on fire, would you call such a person an idiot? You'd probably have a hard time not to. You'd certainly call them mentally ill, would you not?

I'd call them both: an idiot and mentally ill. Well then what is the difference between someone who deliberately sets themself on fire in this world and someone who deliberately sets themself on fire in the next?

Because that's what almost everyone you meet and see in this world is doing. They are literally dousing their eternal souls in gasoline and applying a lit match, with full knowledge that they are condemning themselves to burn forever in the fires of hell.

You might argue that not all of them are doing it will full knowledge. You might say that many of them are ignorant of what they are doing. But are they really? And if they are truly ignorant, wouldn't you then call them idiots for not knowing the truth? They have plenty of time on their hands—much more time than I do. They could turn off the boob tube for five minutes and do a little research into what's going on in the world. But no, they won't do it. Learning and accepting the truth holds less interest for them than the latest soap opera or football game.

St. Paul described such people perfectly in his second epistle to the Thessalonians 2:10 when he wrote: "And in all seduction of iniquity to them that perish: because they receive not the love of the truth that they might be saved. Therefore God should send them the operation of error, to believe lying: That all may be judged who have not believed the truth but have consented to iniquity."

In other words, these are people of such bad will that God allows them to be duped and fooled by liars.

These are the people you saw wearing face masks during the "pandemic." Some of them are still wearing masks. These are the people you see filling the stadiums at sporting events and concerts, the people visiting Las Vegas and Disneyland, the people who blindly believe every lie they see on television. These are the people who surrendered the country without a shot being fired, and willfully injected themselves and their children with a fake vaccine. Are they not all idiots?

I have a hard time feeling sorry for someone like that. I feel sad over their stupidity and I feel sad over the horrible fate that awaits them in hell, and I do feel sorry for their children. But when I see adults acting in this way, collaborating with the enemy and betraying both God and country, it's hard to feel sympathy. I just want to avoid them.

If you want a happy life, and even more importantly, if you want to achieve eternal happiness in Heaven, you must— absolutely must—stay as far away from idiots as you can.

How to Spot an Idiot

Idiots come in all shapes and sizes and judging people by their looks alone can be deceiving. Some idiots are fashion conscious, some aren't. Some idiots appear outwardly friendly, some don't. Some idiots are blissfully ignorant, some are morosely sad. Sometimes the person you least suspect of idiocy turns out to be the biggest idiot of all.

In current time America, you could make the case that anyone who wore a face diaper during the "pandemic" is an idiot and I wouldn't argue with you. Although, I would suggest that exceptions be made for children, teenagers, and even those in their early twenties. They have been duped and lied to by their teachers and many of them honestly don't know any better.

You could also make the case that anyone who took the jab is an idiot. Once again, I wouldn't argue with you except to say that you might want to include the same age limits as before, along with a few rare exceptions. A friend of mine took the jab in order to save his marriage. He knew the score, but decided that the risks—death, paralysis and serious illness—outweighed the alternative—losing his marriage. In his case, it was a carefully considered decision.

If you took the jab, don't fret. We've all been duped and played for fools at one time or another. You wouldn't believe all of the lies I was taught when I was growing up; lies that I believed well into adulthood. It took a lot of reading and a lot of research to sift through those lies and begin to see the truth. And I'm still learning. So don't be too hard on yourself if you did take the jab. At your age, it's not your fault. You were lied to. Read the book *Reversing the Side Effects of the COVID-19 Vaccine: How to Heal Yourself from Adverse Reactions to the Trump Vaccine and Protect Yourself from Shedding*. There's still hope for you. Lots of hope.

How else can you spot an idiot?

Idiots are big-time television watchers. Their favorite programs are soap operas, game shows, professional and college sports, talent competitions, sitcoms, late night talk shows, and the news. If you know an adult who watches television, the odds are that person is an idiot.

Television to an idiot is a mental life preserver. Take away their television and they wouldn't know what to think or what to say about anything. They'd likely suffer withdrawal symptoms similar to a heroin addict.

Idiots repeat what they see on television. Their opinion on any subject is often a word-for-word regurgitation of the last television show they watched. If you ask their opinion about something that hasn't been covered on television, you'll likely be met with a fluoride stare. They won't have an opinion on it, because no one has told them what to think.

Idiots tend to occupy two extremes when it comes to education. They are either uneducated without a high school diploma or highly educated with a college degree. The former group is composed of welfare mothers, non-working males, and generally anyone who depends on government support to survive, while the latter group comprises white-collar professionals and anyone in academia.

Because they belong to these two extremes, idiots are most often found in the following professions: print and broadcast journalism, book publishing, teaching, education, nursing, medicine, corporate management, education administration, the entertainment industry, and working for the government. If you know anyone employed in one of those industries, then most likely that person is an idiot.

Idiots tend to vote Democrat. Not that those who don't vote Democrat are much smarter—there are plenty of idiots in that camp too. But generally those who don't vote Democrat are smart enough to see the rampant crime, crumbling cities, and economic devastation that have resulted from leftwing economic policies, therefore they vote against those policies.

Idiots see the same thing, but shrug it all off. They lack the brain cells needed to comprehend the connection between leftwing government policies and economic collapse. As long as they're getting theirs, they don't care about anyone else.

Idiots are self-centered. They vote for their own self-interests, regardless of the negative consequences for others. They act, often in hysterical and violent fashion, in order to justify their own selfish desires.

Idiots like being lied to. Most people are surprised when they hear this, but they're not surprised when they learn the reason why. Idiots like being lied to because it relieves them of personal responsibility and absolves them of their sins (or so they think). If anything goes wrong, they can claim they were merely "obeying orders" or "following the science."

Idiots prefer comforting lies to uncomfortable truth. Truth forces them to think, an activity that many of them are incapable of. Thus, they gravitate toward others who are as equally dishonest as they are. They are happy to vote known liars into public office.

Idiots are committed to lies. Their self-perception, not to mention their money, their career, and even their marriage very often depends upon continual belief in lies. Think about that one for a minute.

Idiots profess blind faith in authority, yet almost all of them are irreligious. The few that aren't irreligious are either fake Christians or they follow religions of the devil. The ones that claim to be Christian are CINOs—Christians in Name Only. They've been brainwashed to accept the post Vatican II counterfeit church and its line of wicked anti-popes. They call themselves Christian, but their actions are decidedly anti-Christian.

There's only so much you can do with the idiots in your life. I've found that the best approach is to have as little to do with them as possible. That can be difficult as the vast majority of people today are idiots in one way or another. A smart person like you can tolerate them, but only for so long.

Homeschooling is one of the best ways to avoid idiots in your life. For anyone who hasn't graduated high school, it's probably the best way.

I used to feel sorry for idiots and occasionally I still do. But it's almost always young people that earn my sympathy. When I see children and teens forced to live among idiots, it breaks my heart. I wish I could help them, but there's only so much I can do. The idiot adults in their life have made the world a sad place.

Like frogs being slow-boiled in a pot, idiots are oblivious to their own impending destruction. The only difference is the frogs are smarter. Turn up the heat too fast and the frog will catch on and hop right out of the pot. Idiots won't do that. For years now, they've had the heat turned up to scorching hot temperatures in terms of the moral rot of society and the destruction of the country, yet they remain utterly clueless.

I'll be honest with you: it's going to be hard to avoid all the idiots in your life. But you must make your best effort. You can't just throw up your hands and say it can't be done.

Limiting your contact with other people, especially adults, by homeschooling is a great start. It keeps you away from idiot teachers and school administrators.

Let's go back to our analogy of the person dousing themself with gasoline and setting themself on fire. If you knew someone was predisposed to do such a thing, would you spend time with them? No, of course you wouldn't.

Well, the idiots of the world are telling you right to your face that they intend to set themselves on fire. They're telling you with their words and their actions that they are freely accepting eternity in hell. Do you want people like that in your life?

My advice is to avoid them like the plague.

Everyone You Meet Today is Mentally Deranged

The above sentence is what I wrote on a note that I taped to the inside of my front door so I would see it whenever I stepped outside during the fake pandemic and encountered a sea of face-masked zombies. My entire neighborhood, virtually everyone I passed on the street or interacted with in any way, was literally mentally deranged. They still are today.

As you learn more about the reality of life, you'll start to feel the same way. You are going to find yourself to be the lone voice of reason in a sea of idiotic dissent. It's going to appear to you that everyone in your life is mentally deranged and they will be. They will all be operating on false beliefs fueled by the mainstream media. You will be the only one who is actually living in reality.

That's why homeschooling is so important for you at this stage of your life. I suggest you get some information on the subject as soon as possible, study it, and then present it to your parents. There's nothing you can learn in high school or college that you can't learn better on your own at home.

Whether your parents allow you to homeschool or not, one thing you must do as soon as possible is sit down with a school counselor (pick the one who is less of an idiot than all the others) and find out what you need to do in order to graduate in three years instead of four.

Yes, it's possible to do that, to graduate in three years. Find out what the requirements are, and then adjust your life so you are able to complete them. That will shave one year off your time spent in the insane asylum.

In fact, if you're in a big hurry, you can take a GED (General Education Development) test at any age and not even bother with high school.

If you've read this far into this book, then it's obvious that you possess a superior intellect. You could probably take the GED test and pass right now. You can even take practice tests just to make sure.

If you pass the GED, you can then go straight to college, or get to work on making your first million dollars (keeping in mind what we discussed earlier about money).

I wish I had done that when I was sixteen, before my parents threw me out. Only nobody told me. I didn't know such things as a GED test even existed. But now you know.

Don't be put off that it's not an actual diploma. In life, nobody cares about such things. No one will ever ask to see your diploma or your grades.

I've produced and starred in movies, won screenwriting contests, written over twenty books, ran a business, supervised hundreds of employees, and no one has ever asked to see a high school diploma or my grades. If I had brought the subject up, they would have laughed me out of the room.

Unless you're aiming for an academic scholarship, what you achieve in high school means nothing in the real world. So why not get a GED or graduate in three years and kiss the dump goodbye?

You can also graduate from college in three years and if you intend on going to college, you should find out what those requirements are too and plan immediately to fulfill them.

About College

Is college right for you? I know every adult in your life has told you it is, but is it really?

If you think the level of lies you're being told in high school is bad, just wait until you go to college. You'll be hit with a virtual tidal wave of lies and surrounded by so many brainless idiots you'll feel like you've stumbled into a mental ward.

Colleges today are actual indoctrination centers where independent thinking is stamped out and young minds are molded into liberal mush. Spending four years in college is equivalent to getting a lobotomy.

The level of disinformation and stupidity running rampant on college campuses is so high it is simply mind-boggling to comprehend. And for what? Today a college degree is essentially worthless. Over half of the employers in the country now hold it against an applicant if they have a college degree. They know that anyone who spent four years in college has been dumbed down to a point that is irreparable.

Consider college carefully. Aside from the study of law and engineering, there's nothing you can learn in college that you can't learn better on your own.

Congratulations

I have good news for you. If you've read this far and understood what you've read, then you are officially smarter and know more about life than every teacher at your school and just about every adult you'll ever encounter.

Turn to the next chapter for the most important information of all.

Chapter Ten

Saving Your Soul—Nothing Else Matters

Has anyone ever told you to follow your dreams? Have they told you how you can be, do, or have anything you want in life if you work hard and believe you can?

Well, guess what? That's the biggest load of crap you'll ever hear.

In the first place, it's putting your entire focus on the materialistic worldly plane. Life on the worldly plane is shallow and fleeting. What's far more important is where you will spend eternity when you leave this world.

Second of all, there's a huge part to what they're saying that's deliberately missing. What's not said, what's *never* said, is that you can be, do, or have anything you want in life *if you are willing to pay the price.* And of course, no one ever dares to tell you what that price is.

The price to achieving your dreams can range from something as useless and petty as a college degree to losing your very soul.

So if your dreams are small, if all you want to do is graduate college and work for some soulless, multinational corporation, then that type of insipid advice is useful—follow your dreams, work hard, believe you can.

But if your dreams are big, then the price required is far more devastating than you can imagine.

If you want to "make it" in the music business today, you have to sell your soul. I mean that literally. You have to literally sell your soul. Nobody ever talks about that, because most people aren't aware of it. But it's a reality nonetheless. If you want to be famous in the music business, recording albums and playing concerts all over the world, the price you must pay is your own eternal soul.

You can have a lifetime of fame and fortune, an endless parade of girls—a new one every day if you want—as long as you're willing to pay that price.

The movie business isn't much better. You won't be required to literally sell your soul, but you will be required to renounce Christianity and get onboard the anti-white, pro-homosexual, pro-abort bandwagon. You will have to consign yourself to working with the most evil and disgusting people on the planet. Otherwise your career is going nowhere.

Old-timers might tell you differently, but they're living in the past. It was easy when they were starting out. Today the entertainment industry has been completely taken over by sodomite Satanists.

I know, I was in the business for a long time. The reason I quit is because I came to my senses and decided that my eternal salvation is more important than temporary fame and fortune on earth.

Want to be President of the United States? How about Governor of your state? How about a corporate CEO? All of those positions and more are going to require a level of subservience from you. You'll really have to lower yourself. You might even have to grovel. But don't worry, no one will tell as long as you toe the line.

Fame and major success on the earthly plane isn't earned, it's allowed. Yes, you can achieve a certain level of success on your own, provided you have talent. But there are millions of other talented people. If you want to reach the upper echelons of the entertainment industry, or any industry of note, it will require permission from the powerbrokers at the top. You will be forced to compromise your Christian Faith; to bend over and take what the people who run the world demand of you in exchange for the worldly success you desire. If you're willing to pay that price, then you too can be governor, president, or a movie star.

People who say that you can be whatever you want in life if you only work hard and believe you can are so far removed from reality they may as well be living on the funny farm.

Withdraw from the World

Almost everyone you know is going to hell. It's a sobering thought, but it's also true. If you don't want to join them, you're going to have to withdraw from the institutions of society. Almost on one is willing to do that. Almost no one is willing to give up their worldly temptations.

I've been into alternative healing since I was a teenager and have helped hundreds of people heal themselves from every disease imaginable: cancer, arthritis, acne, depression, migraine headaches . . . you name it, I've helped someone heal from it. Whenever a person comes to me with a health issue, the first question I ask is whether they're willing to give up the things that are making them sick. Surprisingly, or maybe not, the answer in almost every case is no. Despite being in excruciating pain, despite dying in some cases, most people are simply not willing to give up their pizza, pretzels, and soda pop.

If people would rather die than stop drinking soda, imagine how much more difficult it is for them to give up worldly pursuits and pleasures in order to escape the torments of hell. They cling to the things of this world. They simply cannot let them go. Yet all of the fame, fortune, and pleasures of this world don't add up to a hill of beans when it comes time to leave this temporary realm and stand before God.

St. Basil said, "One is where he is before God and nothing more, even if he himself and everyone else thinks otherwise."

No one wants to confront the reality that they're living a life of sin and on their way to hell, so they deny it. They put it out of their mind and pretend Heaven and hell don't exist. Or worse, they figure as long as they don't kill anyone they're going to Heaven.

In the case of women having abortions, they think God will overlook the murder of an innocent child and grant them eternal salvation. How deluded and wrong they are.

The institutions of the world are all corrupt. Government, politics, military, law, media, education, entertainment, sports, business, banking, every one of them rotten to the core.

The more you engage and entangle yourself with them, the greater the chances are that you will be sucked down into their web of sin and corruption.

Like I said earlier, I want you to be comfortable. I don't' want you homeless or begging in the street. (I've been homeless, it's no party.) But I also want you to put all of your worldly pursuits second to your pursuit of Heaven.

This is the opposite of what every idiot in your life is telling you. They're advising you, falsely, on how to be successful here on earth. I'm saying don't be like everyone else. Be different. Be one of the few souls who make it to Heaven.

The Catholic Rosary consists of fifteen mysteries. Each of those fifteen mysteries corresponds to a specific grace, such as divine wisdom or contrition for one's sins. Two of those fifteen mysteries are almost identical. They're the only two mysteries that are in any way alike and both of them have to do with detachment and contempt for the world. That right there shows you just how important it is to remove yourself from the things of this world. Yet how many people are willing to do it? Almost none.

St. Anselm said, "If thou wouldst be certain of being in the number of the elect, strive to be one of the few, not one of the many. And if thou wouldst be sure of thy salvation, strive to be among the fewest of the few."

Be among the fewest of the few. The first step in doing that is to withdraw from the world.

It's been said that each of us is the sum total of the five people we spend the majority of our time with. There's a level of truth to that statement. The people you hang out with, your friends, family members, and co-workers, have an enormous impact on your life. Take the five people you spend the most time with, mush them together, and that's you.

Do you find that thought uplifting? I don't and if you don't either, you might be better off spending time alone.

Solitude is where God is found. It's impossible to contemplate God and establish a relationship with Him when you're constantly surrounded by other people. It can only be done in the silence of solitude.

Spending time with other people increases the likelihood that you will end up burning in the fires of hell. Why is that, you ask? Because being around other people makes you susceptible to their corrupting influence.

One of the easiest ways to help ensure your salvation is to avoid the company of other people. And since practically everyone you meet in life is in a state of mortal sin that means avoiding almost everyone.

Over half of the women you pass on the street or interact with in life have had abortions. They've literally murdered their own child, the most evil and disgusting act imaginable. Of the women who haven't yet murdered their own child, a large segment of them support abortion and vote for it to remain legalized.

What this means is that almost every woman you meet is in a state of mortal sin and on their way to hell. Every second you spend with them increases the chances that you will join them in hell.

It's the same with men. Half of the men you pass on the street or interact with in life have impregnated women who went on to have an abortion. The other half spends their time reading and watching pornography, and engaging in all manner of sin. Many of them are homosexual.

In other words, almost every man you meet is also in a state of mortal sin and on their way to hell. And every second you spend with them increases the chances that you will join them in hell.

The solution to that situation is solitude.

Solitude is a sign of intelligence as the more you learn about life, the less you want to be around people.

That includes spending time away from relatives. St. Alphonsus said, "If attachment to relatives were not productive of great mischief Jesus Christ would not have so strenuously exhorted us to estrangement from them. . . . 'A man's enemies shall be they of his own household.' (Mt. 10:36). Relatives are very often the worst enemies of the sanctification of Christians."

Make quiet time for yourself to read and pray.

Stay away from social media.

If you want to go to Heaven, you really have no choice.

Remember the words of St. Anselm that we quoted earlier. He said, "If thou wouldst be certain of being in the number of the elect, strive to be one of the few, not one of the many. And if thou wouldst be sure of thy salvation, strive to be among the fewest of the few."

If those words struck a chord with you; if they hit you in the heart and resonated deeply, then I strongly suggest visiting the website www.MostHolyFamilyMonastery.com

You'll find a wealth of information there that will assist you on your journey to Heaven. Visit that website today. The plain fact of the matter is that you must become a traditional Catholic in order to go to Heaven. The information on that website will show you how to do that. You can also email me for more information. Becoming a traditional Catholic is the most important advice in this entire book.

Summing Up

We've come a long way, you and I, through the pages of this book. Here's a quick summation of what we learned.

Be polite, even and especially if no one else around you is. You'll stand out as a man of class and breeding among a sea of peasants.

When presented with new information, always ask, "Is this true?" and then verify it for yourself. If it's coming from your teachers at school or from television, it is most definitely *not* true.

Don't participate in homosexuality or trannyism under any circumstances. God is calling on you to help save innocent children from the sick and perverted groomers out to sexually molest and mutilate them. No adult in your life is going to do it. They've shown themselves to be cowards who won't lift a finger to help save any child. It's up to you.

Live a life of honesty, even when it's hard.

Kill your television and unplug from all movies, streaming services, and popular music.

Learn how to fight, not only with your fists but also with firearms and with words.

Build your body fast and easy.

Avoid all drugs and alcohol.

Don't enlist in the military under any circumstances.

When trying to attract women, forget about being nice, acting alpha, or asking them on dates. Instead put yourself in a position of status and let them come to you. Eliminate from your interest any girl of a different race, and eliminate from your life any person, male or female, who supports abortion, feminism, homosexuality, trannyism, or any other sin.

Don't chase riches, fame, or other material pursuits.

In order to provide for yourself and your family, practice the three principals of money: give before you receive, do your best at whatever you do, and engage in productive enterprise.

Save as much money as possible, up to 80% of your income if you can.

Never lend or borrow money.

Get out of that dump you call a school and begin homeschooling. Find out what you need to do to graduate in three years and do it. Also, consider getting a GED and leaving high school immediately. Think carefully before going to college. Above all else, save your soul.

Harden yourself.

Use nutrition, exercise, and sleep to harden your body.

Use the other information in this book to harden yourself mentally and emotionally.

Use prayer and the traditional Catholic Faith to harden yourself spiritually and ensure your place in Heaven.

Make yourself tough as nails.

Thank you very much for buying this book!

If you enjoyed it, please leave a review where you bought the book, because people do read them. Even a short, one-sentence review will help.

If you did not enjoy it, please email me with suggestions on how to improve the text.

If you would like clarification about anything you read in this book, or if I can help you in any way, don't hesitate to contact me. Also, if you would like a list of recommended books to read and websites to visit, where you can learn the truth about the world let me know and I will be happy to send a list to you. You can email me here:

Mikestone114@yahoo.com

One of the reasons why the world is suffering so much is because of a lack of leadership. Our so-called leaders have abandoned us and we are essentially on our own. Without a strong man to lead us out of this mess, nothing will change. The people are desperate for leadership, but the strong leader we need is nowhere around. Perhaps it will be you.

Mike Stone is the author of *Based*, a young adult novel about race, dating and growing up in America, and *A New America*, a dark comedy set on Election Day 2016. He has also written the books:

Using ChatGPT & AI to Predict the Future: How to Discern the Truth, Forecast the Future & Always Be Right

Reversing the Side Effects of the COVID-19 Vaccine: How to Heal Yourself from Adverse Reactions to the Trump Vaccine and Protect Yourself from Shedding

5 Stars! This is the fundamental work for all thinking beings. I cannot recommend this book more highly.

COVID-19 and the Mark of the Beast: What Every Christian Needs to Know about the Trump Vaccine.

5 Stars! The author succinctly lays out why no Christian should ever participate in any aspect of the Covid-19 hoax.

COVID-19 and Kids: A Parent's Guide to the COVID-19 Pandemic

Is COVID-19 a Conspiracy?

A New America

On the most divisive day of the year, in the most racially-charged city in America, recently red-pilled movie producer John Duke is about to learn what political correctness really means: marching with the herd or losing everything, including his family.

5 Stars! "A well-written book of an America gone mad."

5 Stars! "More!! Great read!"

5 Stars! "An exciting well-written novel. The author uses no clichés, his descriptions are original, and as a whole the writing is very creative."

5 Stars! "A fast-paced exciting novel."

5 Stars! "Read it all in one sitting. Had to remind myself it's supposed to be fiction."

5 Stars! "I hope this book is read far and wide, because it is the truth."

5 Stars! "You would never see a book written like this in a mainstream publication."

Based

"Ryan Turner was standing alone on the subway platform when he saw the punch coming."

So begins another day of high school in Southern California where teachers attempt suicide, race riots erupt in the cafeteria, and everyone strives to avoid the ultimate in humiliation: diversity training.

A young adult novel about race, dating, and growing up in America.

5 Stars! "Simply off the charts!"

5 Stars! "Couldn't put it down!"

5 Stars! "Sharp and funny take on the upside down world we live in today